KALI LINUX

THE COMPLETE GUIDE TO LEARN LINUX FOR BEGINNERS AND KALI LINUX, LINUX SYSTEM ADMINISTRATION AND COMMAND LINE, HOW TO HACK WITH KALI LINUX TOOLS, COMPUTER HACKING AND NETWORKING.

licensed professional before attempting any techniques outlined in this book.

By reading this document, the reader agrees that under no circumstances is the author responsible for any losses, direct or indirect, which are incurred as a result of the use of information contained within this document, including, but not limited to, errors, omissions, or inaccuracies.

Introduction

When you think of hacking, you may imagine something along the lines of someone violently smashing a keyboard, zooming in on things while controlling someone else's computer, and saying things like "I'm in" or "Hack engaged." Or maybe the word hacking makes you think of breaking into someone's Instagram account.

A History of Hacking

Hacking has been around since as early as the 1960s when, in 1961, a group of MIT students hacked their model trains hacking to modify their functions. That is where the term comes from. So the term hacking is not even directly related to computers! Originally, hacking meant to explore and improve something.

In the 1970s, phone hackers, or "phackers," made their debut when they exploited operational characteristics in phones to gain access to free phone calls, although they were fairly rare. At the time, computer hackers were not yet popular because so few people had personal computers.

This changed in the 1980s when personal computer use gave birth to the first computer hackers. This is no surprise, since when there's a product, there is always someone out there willing to mess with the product to their advantage. Likewise, when there's someone to mess with the product, there is someone to protect it. The birth of computer hacking led to the birth of ethical hacking, as well. The '80s was the decade we first saw hackers breaking into systems to use them for personal gain.

This new type of crime naturally called for new legislation. In 1986, the Federal Computer Fraud and Abuse Act was first written. The Act made it a crime for anyone to access a computer used by a financial institution, a government agency, or any organization involved in foreign commerce or communication. This was mainly prompted by the increase in PC use by the general public.

The 1990s was marked by the first high-profile arrests related to hacking. Kevin Mitnick, Kevin Poulsen, Robert Morris, and Vladimir Levin were among the first to get arrested for stealing property software as well as leading digital heists. This was also when the term crackers, meaning those that "crack" into digital encryption codes (e.g. passwords and such), began to be used.

During the late 2000s, the hacking of major companies like eBay, Amazon, and Microsoft often dominated the headlines. This was particularly true when news broke in early 2000 that the International Space Station's system had been breached by 15-year-old Jonathon James.

1. Ethical Hacker

In the real-world examples, you would call an ethical hacker the firefighter of the group; they put out fires and save innocent lives. They are, more often than not, hired by a government or a law agency to protect data and resolve any harm caused to individuals or businesses. A small business can also hire an ethical hacker to protect the company's data used maliciously or attacked by a malicious hacker.

Unethical Hacker - The Cracker

The unethical hacker, also known as the cracker, is the criminal that gets his information and assets illegally by getting into a device without the owner's knowledge or consent. The intent of this hacking is malicious. This type of hacker causes financial harm, steals confidential data, embezzles funds, disrupts businesses, and spreads incorrect data, among other things.

The Grey Hat

Then there is the hacker who isn't completely ethical or unethical; he's the person that steals to feed the poor. He falls in the gray area between the two other types of hackers. This gray area is where the name grey hat stems from. An example of a grey hat hacker would be a hacker who is hired to protect a particular database and then uses that access to confidential data for personal gain. You may not consider them criminals, but they won't be getting any medals soon. Then you have your "hacktivists," groups such as Anonymous, that use hacking for political and social messages. Finally, there are the "kiddies," or non-skilled people who use already-made tools to gain access to systems. This is when you guess someone's Facebook password because you want to see if they were where they said they were last night.

Types of Hacking

As you can tell, hacking isn't as simple as guessing someone's password and logging into their accounts. There are actually numerous types of hacking that you need to be familiar with.

Phishing

The concept of phishing comes from the everyday activity of fishing. These types of hacks use email or sometimes phone to pose as a legitimate institution to obtain important information that can hurt an individual or a business. Hence, they throw the hook to "fish" for a victim. This usually works by first telling the victim they're a trusted organization, then asking for confidential data.

The first phishing lawsuit was filed in 2004 against a Californian teenager who created a copy of the website called "America Online" where he retrieved credit card information from visitors. One of the first and most popular phishing emails was the infamous "Nigerian Prince" email, which was an email from a "prince" who was stuck and needed your help to get back to his millions. Today, most of us don't fall for the Nigerian Prince scam, but phishing is still alive and problem for millions of internet users. The prevalent phishing - emails are mostly easy to spot. They share a sense of urgency, unusual sender and suspicious hyperlinks. It is when a website is copied and looks like the real thing that things can get complicated. Banking websites can often be targets of phishing because of their extensive access to credit card numbers and sensitive information.

Virus

The purpose of a virus is to corrupt resources on websites. Just like in a human body, the virus can change forms, corrupt the "healthy" programs, and self-propagate. And just like in with us, there are plenty of viruses that can attack your malware.

Topher Crypter Virus is one of the most dangerous types of viruses because of its ability to completely take over the computer, leading to the spread of further viruses. A famous example of a Topher Crypter is the Trojan Virus.

Metamorphic Virus can write, rewrite, and edit its own code. It is the most infectious virus, and it can do massive damage to the computer and data if not detected early.

Polymorphic Virus is similar to a metamorphic virus, but it copies itself; where the metamorphic virus can rewrite its code, the polymorphic just copies its original code with slight modifications.

Macro Virus is written in the same language as software programs such as Microsoft Word or Excel. It starts an automatic sequence of actions every time the application is opened.

Cluster Virus makes it appear as though every program in the system is affected when, in fact, it is only in the one program in the system. It causes the illusion of a cluster and can be removed by figuring out the original "carrier" of the virus.

Tunneling Virus works against antiviruses. It sits in the background and sits under the antivirus. When an antivirus detects virus, the antivirus will try to re-install itself only to install itself as the tunneling viruses.

Stealth Virus uses its mechanism to avoid any detection by antiviruses. The stealth virus will hide in the memory and hide any changes it has made to any files.

Extension Virus will hide in a website or browser extension and create changes through there.

Cookie Theft

Cookies are files stored on your computer used by your browser to save useful information about the websites you visit or any actions you take. Session cookies are temporary and erased once you close your browser. Certain cookies persist in your browser until you yourself erase them or they expire (which could take years). These are called persistent cookies.

Websites use cookies to modify your browsing experience in order to make it tailored to your needs as well as for proper ad placement. Cookie thefts are used by hackers in order to gain access to that information. Cookies are one of the most natural methods of hacking, they can be stolen through public Wi-Fi networks!

UI Redress

UI redress, also called clickjacking, is masking a click in order to gain clicks for a different website. A user might think they are clicking on a straightforward link, but due to clickjacking, they will be redirected to a completely different website. The hacker is "hijacking" clicks. This can get out of control quickly as users will click links that say things such as "win a free vacation," and they will be redirected to a sharing page, causing the clickjacking to spread massively over social media or email.

DNS Spoofing

Domain name server spoofing is an attack in which the domain name is taken over by redirecting the clicks to a fraudulent website. Once there, the users are led to believe they are logging in with their account names and passwords into the original website, but in reality, they are giving away their information to the hacker performing the DNS spoofing. There are a few methods to perform DNS spoofing such as Man in the Middle (where interaction among the server and user is sidetracked) or DNS server compromise (where the server is directly attacked).

The above examples are all types of hacking used by malicious hackers, but ethical hacking also works with them. In order to prevent and "heal" these attacks, the ethical hackers must know how they work, and this is why ethical hackers have to be educated on all the types and methods of hacking used.

Becoming a hacker takes skill, and the ironic part is that both unethical and ethical hackers will use the same education and tools. The only difference is that one will use their "powers" for evil and the other for good (or something in between). It's like a modern-day equivalent of the classic superhero-villain duo Batman and Joker. In order to be a successful ethical hacker, you have to understand malicious hacking as well.

2. The Meaning of Ethical Hacking And Types

Ethical Hacking is an approved routine with regards to bypassing framework security to distinguish potential information ruptures and dangers in a system. The organization that claims the framework or system permits Cyber Security specialists to perform such exercises so as to test the framework's safeguards. In this manner, not at all like pernicious hacking, this procedure is arranged, affirmed, and all the more significantly, legitimate.

Ethical programmers plan to examine the framework or system for powerless focuses that pernicious programmers can abuse or decimate. They gather and break down the data to make sense of approaches to fortify the security of the framework/organize/applications. Thusly, they can improve the security impression so it can all the more likely withstand assaults or redirect them.

The act of Ethical hacking is designated "White Hat" hacking, and the individuals who perform it are called

White Hat programmers. As opposed to Ethical Hacking, "Dark Hat" hacking portrays works on including security infringement. The Black Hat programmers utilize unlawful procedures to bargain the framework or obliterate data.

Not at all like White Hat programmers, "Dim Hat" programmers don't request authorization before getting into your framework. Be that as it may, Gray Hats are additionally not quite the same as Black Hats since they don't perform hacking for any close to home or outsider advantage. These programmers don't have any malevolent expectation and hack frameworks for entertainment only or different reasons, more often than not advising the proprietor about any dangers they find. Dark Hat and Black Hat hacking are both unlawful as the two of them establish an unapproved framework break, despite the fact that the goals of the two sorts of programmers vary.

The most ideal approach to separate between White Hat and Black Hat programmers is by investigating their intentions. Dark Hat programmers are inspired by malevolent goal, showed by of individual increases, benefit, or provocation; though White Hat programmers search out and cure vulnerabilities, in order to keep Black Hats from exploiting.

Different approaches to draw a differentiation between White Hat and Black Hat programmers include:

Procedures utilized: White Hat programmers copy the strategies and techniques pursued by malevolent programmers so as to discover the framework inconsistencies, recreating all the last's means to discover how a framework assault happened or may happen. On the off chance that they locate a powerless point in the framework or system, they report it quickly and fix the imperfection.

Lawfulness: Even however White Hat hacking pursues indistinguishable procedures and strategies from Black Hat hacking, just one is legitimately worthy. Dark Hat programmers violate the law by entering frameworks without assent.

Possession: White Hat programmers are utilized by associations to enter their frameworks and identify security issues. Dark cap programmers neither possess the framework nor work for somebody who claims it.

Jobs and Responsibilities of an Ethical Hacker

Ethical Hackers must pursue certain rules so as to perform hacking legitimately. A decent programmer knows their obligation and clings to the majority of the Ethical rules. Here are the most significant principles of Ethical Hacking:

An Ethical programmer must look for approval from the association that possesses the framework. Programmers ought to acquire total endorsement before playing out any security appraisal on the framework or system.

Decide the extent of their evaluation and make known their arrangement to the association.

Report any security breaks and vulnerabilities found in the framework or system.

Keep their revelations secret. As their motivation is to verify the framework or system, Ethical programmers ought to consent to and regard their non-divulgence understanding.

Eradicate all hints of the hack in the wake of checking the framework for any defenselessness. It keeps malignant programmers from entering the framework through the distinguished provisos.

Ethical Hacking is a difficult territory of concentrate as it requires dominance of everything that makes up a framework or system. This is the reason affirmations have turned out to be well known among yearning Ethical programmers.

With applicable Ethical Hacking confirmations, you can propel your vocation in cybersecurity in the accompanying ways:

Confirmed people realize how to configuration, fabricate, and keep up a safe business condition. In the event that you can exhibit your insight in these zones, you will be precious with regards to examining dangers and formulating successful arrangements.

Ensured cybersecurity experts have better pay prospects contrasted with their non-confirmed friends. As per Payscale, Certified Ethical Hackers procure a normal compensation of $90K in the U.S.

Confirmation approves your aptitudes in the field of IT security and makes you progressively detectable while applying for testing work jobs.

With the developing occurrences of security breaks, associations are putting gigantically in IT security and lean toward affirmed contender for their association.

New companies need profoundly talented experts experienced in repulsing digital dangers. A confirmation can enable you to show your IT security abilities to acquire lucrative occupations at new businesses.

In this day and age, cybersecurity has turned into a drifting subject of expanding enthusiasm among numerous organizations. With noxious programmers discovering more current approaches to break the barriers of systems consistently, the job of Ethical programmers has turned out to be progressively significant over all parts. It has made a plenty of chances for cybersecurity experts and has motivated people to take up Ethical hacking as their profession. Along these lines, on the off chance that you have ever thought about the potential outcomes of getting into the cybersecurity space, or even simply upskilling, this is the ideal time to do as such. What's more, obviously the most proficient method for achieving this is by getting guaranteed in Ethical hacking, and the most ideal approach to do that is to let Simplilearn help you accomplish it! Look at them now, and join the battle for secure frameworks

3. Pick Your Hat

Remember in the *Harry Potter* series when the sorting hat sorts you into which house you're supposed to be in (Slytherin for the bad ones, Gryffindor for the brave ones, etc.). Hacking hats are similar to this, only you're your own sorting hat, and you can switch sides. Let's learn what each means.

To understand the hats hackers metaphorically wear, we must first understand the ethical standards in the hacker communities.

Hacker Ethics

Richard Stallman of the Free Software Foundation, as well as one of the creators of the copyleft concept had the following to say about hacking:

"The hacker ethic refers to the feelings of right and wrong, to the ethical ideas this community of people had—that knowledge should be shared with other people who can benefit from it, and that important resources should be utilized rather than wasted."

The general principles of hacker ethics are:

1. Access to computers must be universal and unlimited

2. All information must be free

3. Encourage decentralization

4. Judge, according to hacks, not according to diplomas, economic stance, race, gender, religion, etc.

5. Create art and beauty with computers

6. Change your life for the better

Black Hat Hacker

The term black hat hacker is derived from old Western movies where the bad guys wore black hats, and the good guys wore—you guessed it—white hats.

The freshest looking color black gets all the bad rap. Villains often wear only black, and then there's death, dark magic and black cats—all associated with dark and evil things. Black hat hackers are thus the ones we hear about in the media the most, the ones using their "powers" for evil.

The black hat hacker is the one that finds security flaws to gain access and uses them for their malicious intents. These can be financial—such as gaining information about credit cards so you can access assets and accounts—or purely informational. Black hat hackers gain access to personal files of celebrities, and they are the ones that will go shopping with your card or even access files from large corporations for larger-scale hacks. Black hat hackers can cause significant damage to an individual or a business, compromising a website or even shutting down security systems.

Black hat hackers range from a kid spreading viruses to major league hackers obtaining credit card passwords. Sometimes, malicious hackers work outside the internet and obtain information through phones by calling and pretending to be a legitimate company. One of the infamous non-computer scams hackers use is pretending to be the IRS or CRS and calling people threatening to take legal action because they haven't paid their taxes. A good rule of thumb to recognize spot this scam is to look for a sense of urgency, like—it has to be paid right here, right now, through your credit card—and the instalment of fear—"if you don't pay this right now you will go to jail!"

Black hat hackers have their conventions, like Comic Con but for hacking. The two famous ones are DefCon and Black Hat. These conventions, however, are often attended by white hat hackers, as well, to learn from the black hats and gain information on anything necessary to know. It's fascinating how close these two worlds have to stay to learn from each other to take each other down.

There are plenty of notorious black hat hackers to choose from, but some stand out even amongst the crowd. Of course, many of the best never got caught, but among those who did get caught are:

Albert Gonzales - He has been accused of the most significant ATM theft in history in the years between 2005 and 2007. When he was arrested, the authorities found $1.6 million cash in his possession as well as $1 million cash around his property, so naturally, he has been sentenced to 20 years in federal prison.

Vladimir Levin - He transferred $10 million from Citibank bank accounts to his own all while hanging out in his apartment. He was discovered when his accomplices tried to withdraw funds from different bank accounts around the world and pointed to him when they were caught. He was arrested and tried for merely three years, and most of the funds have been recovered (apart from $40,000). Media portrayed Levin as a biochemist and a scientist with a Ph.D., but in the later years, it was revealed he was an administrator with not much formal education. Goes to show how sensationalistic it can all get with no actual evidence.

George Hotz - In 2007, at just 17, he was the first person to unlock the iOS security system, and in 2010 he hacked into the Sony system, which resulted in a massive and famous Sony lawsuit. This resulted in the hacking group Anonymous hacking Sony and the most costly security break up to date. He continued to release jailbreak technology up until 2010 when he finally crossed over to the white hat side or more of a gray area.

Johnathan James (aka c0mrade) - At 16 years old, Johnathan became the first person in the United States to go to juvenile prison for cybercrime. At the age of 15, he had broken into the security systems of NASA and the Department of Homeland Defense and stole a software worth over $1 million. He broke into the Defense Threat Reduction Agency and intercepted messages from employees. Johnathan committed suicide at 28, and a past suicide note indicated it may have had something to do with him being implicated in another hacking situation.

Gary McKinnon - McKinnon, from Scotland, hacked into NASA, the US Army, the Air Force, and the Navy systems searching for information about UFOs that he believes the US government is hiding. At one point, a message appeared on all of the computers in the US Army saying "your security system is crap." He has been accused of the largest ever hack of United States government computers, but he was never extradited to the US. The reasons for not doing so was his Asperger's syndrome. Theresa May believed extraditing him would cause more harm than good and that the extradition would be a breach of human rights.

Kevin Mitnick - He started hacking at age 12 by bypassing the punch system in the Los Angeles public bus system. In 1979, at age 17, he gained access to its unauthorized network; following that, he was convicted and sentenced to prison before being given supervised discharge. When he was nearing the end of his probation, he hacked into Pacific Bell computers and fled. He became a fugitive for two and a half years. After a very public pursuit, he was arrested in 1995 on several counts of wire fraud and possession of unauthorized devices. He has been depicted in several movies, books, and comic books, and to this day, he is the most famous black hat hacker.

Hacker Hierarchy

Much like the rest of the world, the hacker world has its own divisions. One of those divisions within the black hat hacker community is based on your hacking skills:

Newbies - They have access to hacker tools but are not very aware of how the programs work.

Cyberpunks - Also known as Green Hat Hackers, they are newbies with more ambition to become coders. They use other tools, but they actively learn to code.

Coders - These are the people who write the programs other hackers use to infiltrate systems.

Cyberterrorists - They infiltrate systems to profit illegally; they are at the top of the hacker food chain.

White Hat Hacker

White hat hackers are what they call the good guys of the hacking industry. They break into systems and do pretty much the same things the black hat hackers do, only the reason behind white hacker hacks is security. They expose vulnerabilities to create higher standards of security before the black hat hackers can take advantage of the system's weaknesses

Often, a former black hat hacker turns white-hat hacker, but you rarely see the opposite. White hat hackers are also known as ethical hackers. In the simplest terms, an ethical hacker tests security networks by pretending to be a malicious hacker to see where the weaknesses are. This means anything from emailing the staff to ask for passwords to testing complicated security systems. This is the reason many black hat hackers switch sides, they get to do the same thing but without the fear of legal prosecution.

Ethical hacking is evident in the US military as well. One of the first instances of ethical hacking was actually conducted by the US Air Force. The idea of ethical hacking didn't come from the Air Force, however. Dan Farmer and Wietse Venema, two programmers, first created the idea of ethical hacking, even if they didn't call it that. Their idea was to raise security on the internet as a whole. Farmer started a software called Computer Oracle and Password System (COPS) designed to identify security weaknesses. Venema designed a Security Administrative Tool for Analyzing Networks (SATAN) that became an accepted method for auditing computer and network security.

Other famous ethical hackers include:

Kevin Mitnick - Yes, the same Kevin Mitnick that was a fugitive is now a famous white hat hacker. After his infamous black hat days, he now works as a consultant and for the FBI. He also acts as a public speaker and teaches classes in universities.

Joanna Rutkowska - She is a cybersecurity researcher focused on Qubes OS. In 2006, she attended a black hat conference and exposed vulnerabilities in Vista Kernel. In 2009, she prevented an attack targeting Intel systems including the Trusted Execution Technology.

Charlie Miller - He is known for exposing vulnerabilities in Apple as well as being the first to locate MacBook Air bug. He spent years working for Uber, and at some point, he even worked for the National Security Agency

(NSA). In 2014 he hacked a Jeep Cherokee and managed to control its brakes, steering wheel and acceleration remotely.

Greg Hoglund - He is an author, researcher, and specialist in computer forensics. He contributed to software exploitation and online game hacking and has patented methods for fault injections for white hat hacking purposes. He also founded the popular rootkit.com, a website devoted to the subject of rootkits (collection of computer software designed to enable access that is not otherwise allowed). White hat hackers have a harder job and get a lot less credit, but the work they do is a lot more fulfilling and, in the end, legal. While as a black hat hacker some get "cool points," white hat hacking is as equally as interesting. The coolest thing about white hat hacking is all the freedom you get to enjoy because you're not being prosecuted and arrested.

Grey Hat Hackers

Nothing is black and white, and neither are the hacker hats. There is a group of hackers who fall between black and white hackers, called grey hat hackers. So what exactly are grey hat hackers?

They are the hackers who won't always abide by the laws or ethical standards, but they don't have the malicious intents that the black hat hackers do. The term was first coined at a black hat convention DEFCON by a hacker group L0pht, and it was first publicly used in a New York Times interview in 1999.

Lopht described themselves as a group who support the ethical reporting and exposing vulnerabilities but disagree with the full disclosure practices that dominate the white hat communities.

They were also referred to as white hat hackers by day and black hat hackers by night.

It is still not clear as to what a grey hat hacker is because the term is so broad. The general idea is that it is a hacker who will break the law to improve security. You can think of them as the chaotic good of the group.

Some examples of grey hackers are:

Dmitry Sklyarov - In the early 2000s, the Russian citizen, along with his employer, ElcomSoft, caught the attention of the FBI for an alleged violation of the DMCA

(Digital Millennium Copyright Act). Sklyarov visited the US to give a presentation called eBooks Security and was arrested on his way back because he had violated the DMCA. The complaint was that Sklyarov and his company illegally obtained copy protection arrangements by Adobe. The US government eventually dropped all charges against him in exchange for his testimony against ElcomSoft.

Julian Assange - Julian Assange, the creator of WikiLeaks, a non-profit that publishes news leaks, is perhaps the clearest example of a grey hat hacker. He began hacking at age 16 and went on to hack NASA, the Pentagon, and Stanford University. He created WikiLeaks in 2006, and it remains an ethical grey area. Some argue that Assange is merely exposing the corruption of elite corporations, while others argue that the work he is doing is illegal and corrupt. One of the most notorious documents released by WikiLeaks is the video of US soldiers shooting 18 civilians from a helicopter in Iraq. Assange has been fleeing the law for years, and he is currently. He is being charged on 17 different counts, and many argue the charges are not valid and a symbol of the end of free journalism.

Loyd Blankenship - Also known as the The Mentor, Blankenship is a well-known writer and hacker. He was a member of different hacker groups including the Legion of Doom. He is the author of the *Hacker Manifesto* and *GURPS Cyberpunk*, which is a cyberpunk roleplaying sourcebook written for Steve Jackson Games. That book landed Blankenship in hot water because it was believed he illegally accessed Bell South and that this would help other groups commit similar hacks.

Guccifer - Guccifer is a Romanian hacker that targeted celebrities. He was the man behind the Hillary Clinton email leak that some argue ultimately caused her downfall in the 2016 presidential elections and got Donald Trump elected. Before Clinton, Guccifer accessed the emails of Romanian starlets. He then moved onto US Secretary of State Colin Powel and George W. Bush.

Anonymous - This is a well-known hacktivist group that has been in the news recently. They are widely known for their attacks against government agencies, institutions, corporations, and the Church of Scientology, but the Anonymous resume list can go on for days. Several people have been arrested for involvement in Anonymous cyberattacks, but to this day, the group still operates.

Hacker hats are all about what you ultimately want to stand for. The idea is the same—penetrate security measures made by individuals and companies. The ethical standpoint behind the hacking decides which hat you want to choose for yourself.

If you are just looking to have some fun testing systems, then stick with the clear-cut white hat hacking. I mean, stick with it in general because it will keep you out of jail.

4. Programming Linux

Programming on Linux is being used for creating interfaces, applications, software and programs. Linux code is often used for the desktop, embedded systems as well as for real-time programs. Linux is an open source OS kernel which is compatible with Perl, C++, Java and various other languages of programming.

How does Linux work?

Linux functions as the kernel of an OS which can also be distributed and shared freely. An operating system or OS is that interface which helps in connecting the users with the hardware of computer and also supports the running of the applications and programs. Kernel is nothing but the OS core as it manages all the communication between the components of hardware and software.

What are the functions of the Linux programmers?

Starting off with Linux programming employ tools such as GBU compiler and also debugger which helps in creating applications for the storage of data, construction of GUI and also script writing. More advanced form of applications related to Linux allows the programmers to develop software related to Linux, optimize the programs which are already existing and also write new programs with various complex form of features such as multiprocessing, multi-threading, inter-process communication and also interaction of hardware device.

Uses of Linux

Linux is being widely used today in various servers, system of computer security and architecture of computer system. It is also widely used in the real-time programs along with the embedded systems of the PDAs and cell phones. Linux programming has also resulted in various applications.

How to develop the modules of Kernel?

Right before you start off with core programming in Linux, the best way of increasing your knowledge along with expertise of Linux programming is to start working on the kernel module. The modules are developed independently which works with the Linux kernels for functioning as a compact operating system. The kernel modules consist of various things such as drivers of devices for the several peripheries of hardware, file managers and other low-level features of the OS. The only barrier that comes at the entry of kernel module is much lower in rate than there are for working on the kernel of Linux. There are several modules which are being developed by various individuals and teams. So, it can be concluded that there is no specific gatekeeper at the entry of development.

Logical Breakdown of Programming in Linux

When you are using some of the major forms of operating system then you are interacting indirectly to the shell. If you are using Linux Mint, Ubuntu or any other proper distribution of Linux, you will be interacting with the shell every single time when you will be using the terminal. Let us discuss about the breakdown of programming in Linux which consists of Linux shells along with scripting of shell. So, right before we start, you will need to get acquainted with some of these terminologies:

- *Kernel*
- *Shell*
- *Terminal*

What is a kernel?

Kernel is nothing but a program related to computer systems which act as the core of the operating system. It comes with overall control over all the elements in a system. It helps in managing various resources of the systems based on Linux:

- Management of files

- Management of processes

- Management of I/O.

- Management of memory

- Management of the devices and various other components

A complete system of Linux can be broken down like: Kernel + installation scripts + other scripts of management + GNU system libraries and utilities.

What is a shell?

A shell is a special type of user program which helps in providing a proper interface to the users for using the services related to an operating system. The shells accept commands which are readable by humans from the users and then converts those into something which can be understood by the kernel. It can be regarded as the interpreter of command language which helps in executing the commands which are read from the devices of input like keyboard or from the files in the system. A shell starts when a user logs into the system or starts with a terminal.

A shell can be easily classified into two different categories:

- *Graphical shell*
- *Command line shell*

The graphical shells provide various means for the purpose of manipulating the programs which are based on the GUI or graphical user interface by letting the operations like closing, opening, resizing and moving windows, along with switching the focus in between the windows. Ubuntu OS along with Windows OS can be regarded as great examples which provide the GUI to the users for the purpose of interacting with various programs.

Shells can be accessed by the users by using the CLI or command line interface. A special type of program in Linux known as the terminal is provided for typing in the commands of the humans like ls, cat and many others and further which are being executed. The final result is then displayed directly on the terminal which can be seen by the user. Suppose you execute the command ls along with the option –l. This will be listing all the available files within the present working directory in a form of long listing.

Working along with the command line shell might turn out to be a bit difficult if you are a beginner only because of the fact that it is tough to memorize a bunch of commands at the same time. It is highly powerful in nature and it also allows the users to store all the commands within a specific file and then execute all of them together. In this way, any form of repetitive task can be made automatic easily. All of these files are generally known as Shell Scripts in the Linux systems.

In a Linux system, there are various types of shells which are available for the users:

• BASH: Also known as Bourne Again Shell, it is being widely used in the systems which are based on Linux. It is being used as the default shell of login in the Linux systems. If you want you can also install this in the Windows operating system.

- CSH: Also known as the C shell, it uses the syntax of the C shell and its usage is more or less similar to the programming language of C.

- KSH: Also known as the Korn shell, it is the base of the POSIX Shell standard.

Each of the shells functions in the same way but all of them understand various commands and also provides various built-in functions.

Scripting of Shell

In general, the shells are interactive in nature which means that they can accept the commands as inputs from the users and can also execute the same. However, it might happen that you need to or want to execute a whole bunch of commands in a routine manner, so you will need to type all the commands every time within the terminal. As the shells can also take in the commands in the form of inputs from the files, you can also write the commands within a file and then execute the same in the shell for avoiding the task of repetition. All these files are known as Shell Programs or Shell Scripts. The shell scripts are somewhat similar in structure with the batch file which can be found in MS-DOS. Each of the shell scripts is saved with the extension of .sh file such as yourscript.sh.

The shell scripts also come with syntax like all other languages of programming. In case you are already acquainted with any of the languages of programming like C, C++ or Python, it will be easier for you to start with shell scripting. The shell scripts consist of:

• Shell Keywords: It includes else, if, break and many others

• Shell Commands: It includes ls, cd, echo, touch, pwd and many others

• Control Flow: It includes if..then..else, shell and case loops and many others

You can use shell scripts for avoiding the repetitive work and thus opting for automation. It also helps in monitoring of the system. It also allows the addition of various new functionalities to the shells.

Programming in Linux Using C

Linux is turning out to be a heaven of programming for all the developers. It is mainly because of the open source nature of Linux and also being a completely free operating system. Turbo C compiler is the old form of compiler which has been used for compiling programs. The same job can be done on Linux for creating a new environment of programming. Let's have a look at how to get started with programming in Linux by using C for writing, compiling and running programs based on C.

Programming in Linux using C++

C can be regarded as a language of programming which is of procedural nature. It was developed in between 1969 and 1973 by Dennis Ritchie. Initially, it was developed as a programming language for the systems for the purpose of writing up a complete operating system. The main features of the C++ language come with low-level accessing of system memory, a very simple and easy set of keywords and a very clean style. All these features make the C++ language very much suitable for all sort of system programming such as operating system or even development of compiler. The very first step includes installation of some tools of development along with several applications like GCC, GNU, C++ compiler for the task of compiling the program and for executing the overall code in Linux. C and C++ are somewhat similar and for understanding C++ let us first have a look at C.

If you want you can also verify the installed set of tools by using the command:

cc −v.

Let us now consider a very easy C program file which is named as Sort.c:

```
int main( void )

{

 printf( "Hello! Sort\n" );

return 0;

}
```

For compiling this easy program you can use:

cc filename.c -0 executable_file_name

In this command, the filename.c is the C program file and -0 option has been used for showing up the errors in the code. In case there is no form of error in the code, it will generate an executable form of file named as executable_file_name.

cc Sort.c -0 sortoutput

In this, sortoutput is the file which is executable in nature and it is being generated. So, you can execute the same like:

./sortoutput

For program files related to C++

C++ is a programming language which has been developed for the general purpose of programming and is being widely used today for the purpose of competitive programming. It comes with object-oriented, imperative and generic program features. You can run C++ on various OS platforms such as Linux, Windows, Mac, Unix and many others. Right before we start programming by using C++ you will be needing a proper environment which needs to be set up on your computer system for the purpose of compiling and running your C++ based programs successfully. You can verify all your installed tools on C++ by using this command:

g++ -- version

Let us consider a very simple C++ program:

```cpp
// main function

// where the execution

// of program starts

int main()

{

// print Hello Universe!

cout<< "Hello Universe!\n";

return 0;

}
```

For compiling this entire code you can use:

g++ filename.cpp -0 executable_file_name

Here in this command, filename.cpp is the file of C++ program and -0 option has been used for showing out the errors within the code. In case no error has been found, it will generate an executable form of file named as executable_file_name.

g++ sort.cpp -0 sortoutput

Here in this command, sortoutput is the executable form of file which is being generated. So, you can execute the same such as:

./sortoutput

Installing compiler for C++ in Linux

If you are using Linux based system such as CentOS, Red Hat, Fedora or something else, you can type in this command as the root for installing the compiler of C++:

yum install –y gcc-c++*

In order to verify that the compiler of GCC has been installed properly in the system use:

rpm –qa | grep –i c++

You can also use the which command as:

which c++

Writing the first C++ based program on Linux

- *From the terminal window, open up a new file for the purpose of editing by using the command vim as:*

vim hello.cc

- *Within the vim editor, you can now type your C++ program or code.*
- *After you are done with writing the program, save and then exit the file.*
- *For compiling the new program of C++, you will need to type this command in the terminal:*

c++ hello.cc

If the compilation process runs without any error, no form of output is going to be printed on the screen.

- *An executable form of file will be created within the present directory with a.out as the default name.*
- *For running this same program, you can execute the executable file which has been generated in a similar way you execute any of the executables of Linux.*

How to specify name meant for the executable which has been generated?

Compiling the programs of C++ without any of the specifying options will be producing an executable form of file with the name a.out. In case you want to specify a particular name for the executable of your choice you have two ways: first, is to rename the a.out default after it has been created and second, is to specify the filename of the executable at the time of compilation by using the option –o.

c++ hello.cc –o /opt/hello.run

Executing the system commands from programs of C++

It is very much important to be able to communicate with the compiling system by executing the commands of OS when needed. The system() function will be allowing you to run the commands of the system from the code of C++. For the ease of the compiler to recognize all these functions properly and for compiling in the proper way, stdlib.h library file is required to be invoked.

Bottom line

- *For writing down C or C++ based programs on the machines based on Linux, you will need the GCC compiler.*
- *All the C++ programs are saved and written as .cc format of files.*
- *All the resulting form of executable can also be executed in a similar way the Linux or Unix executables are being executed.*

- *The system function is being used for running the commands of the system from the code of C++.*
- The g++ and c++ command both compile and link with the source files of C++.

Programming in Linux Using Python

For appending any of the items to the bottom of the list use append(). For removing any of the items from the list, you can easily pass the particular element to the method remove() or the proper position of the item in the list as pop(). For displaying the complete list of the available methods for any object you can use Ctrl+space after you have typed in the item name along with a dot.

Programming in Linux Using Java

Java is one of the most popular languages of programming which is being widely used for the purpose of developing software for almost everything starting from cell phones to the cable TV boxes and extending its use to the large systems of enterprise information. The overall concept behind writing the source code of Java, compiling the same and then running it is more or less the same across most of the OS.

Java is a programming language which was originally developed by the Sun Microsystems. It falls under the category of compiled form of programming language in which the programmer writes up the source code and then submits the same to the compiler which will be checking out the syntaxes of the program and will generate a complete file which you can run. For instance, when you are using Google Chrome web browser, you are in true sense running all the programs which have been generated from a compiler which is used by the software developers.

To a wide extent, the programming languages of the past needed you to re-compile all the source code for every new OS in which you wanted to run your program on. For instance, a program which has been compiled for running in Windows will not be running on a system which has Linux in it unless and until if it has been re-compiled. Given the wide differences in the OS and the elements of hardware, this process was very difficult and complicated to carry out. One of the major motivations for the programming language of Java was the motivation of being able to write only one single set of source code and then provide the resulting program with the ability to run on some different set of operating systems or environments of operation.

Java comes with write once and then run anywhere capability only because of the way in which the compiler translates the entire source code in a particular file known as Byte Code file which can then run under any form of supported JRE or Java Runtime Environment.

The development process of Java involves these steps:

- Write down the Java source code and then save the same in one or more than one plain text files. All of these files generally come with .java format at the end.

- Run the compiler of Java (javac) for compiling the source code which you have written into a file of Byte Code. The Byte Codes generally have .class at end of the name of the file.

- Run the program after submitting the byte code to a JRE.

Downloading Java Development Kit

5. The Hacking Process

The hacking process generally involves coming up with a plan on how the attack will take place. For starters, you should come up with a plan on how to collect information that will come in handy when facilitating the attack. The main importance of the plan is to ensure that the attack will be well-coordinated and there will be no mishaps in the process. Also, the plan ensures that the ethical hacker is confident about what they are doing. The ethical attackers also handle their duties very seriously. For starters, you may start by testing a program that is present on the client's computer; in the process, you may also outline, define, and document your goals. The testing phase is important since you will be able to come up with the testing standards and you will also gain some familiarity with the tools that you are supposed to use during the ethical hacking process. In this chapter, we will also investigate how a good hacking environment can be created since it will help to ensure that the hacking process will be successful. Ethical hackers cannot hack into a system without the authorization of the target or client.

Coming Up with Your Goals

Hackers should come up with goals that are implementable. As an ethical hacker, your main goal is to make sure that you have discovered all the vulnerabilities that are present within the system. If there are any vulnerabilities, the ethical hacker will then come up with techniques that will be used to seal all the loopholes so that the external attackers cannot hack into the system and corrupt it in different ways. The goal formation process involves the following steps:

1. Always define your specific goals. The goals should also align with the objectives of the business/client. As an ethical hacker, make sure that you have investigated the goals that the management is trying to achieve as well as your end-goals.

2. Make sure that you have also formulated a schedule that will guide you from the start to the end of the project. The hacking timeline should also comprise of specific dates and time. For instance, some attacks cannot take place during business hours since there is a lot of traffic because of the employees and a DoS

(Denial of Service) attack should be avoided through all means possible.

The goal formation process may take a lot of time; however, it will be worth it. The goals are meant to offer some guidance. As an ethical hacker, you may also refer to your goals from time to time to ensure that you are on the right track.

Determining the Specific System that You Will Hack

There may be many web applications that should be tested and they cannot be tested at a go since the system may crash in the process. Make sure that the hacking project has been broken down accordingly so that the attack may also be easily manageable. You may also start by carrying out an analysis so that you can be able to investigate the specific systems that you will test first. The main questions that you should ask yourself include:

1. Which systems are critical? There are some systems that can be accessed without the need of any authorization and that means that when an

external attacker gets hold of these systems, there will be a lot of trouble and the business may also incur some losses.

2. Which systems can be attacked easily?
3. Which specific systems have not been documented?

After you have formulated your goals, you will be able to decide the specific systems that you will start to test. The main reason why goals are important is because they will help you to actualize your expectations and you will be able to investigate whether they are achievable. Also, the goals will help you to make sure that you can come up with a timeline and you will also estimate the amount of resources that you need when performing the attack.

The devices that you can test include:

1. Switches and Routers - The switches usually connect the computers on one network. The routers will also connect many networks together.
2. Web applications and database servers.
3. Firewalls.
4. E-mails and files.
5. Bridges and wireless access points.

6. Laptops, workstations, and tablets.

7. Client and server operating systems.

8. The mobile devices are used to store confidential pieces of information.

When dealing with a small network, you can easily test everything. You can test the emails and the web servers. Also, make sure that the ethical hacking process is also flexible. Make sure that you have started with the networks and systems that are highly vulnerable. Some of the factors that you should consider include:

1. The applications that are present within the system.

2. The operating system that is being used.

3. The amount of sensitive information that has been stored within the system and network.

The Attack Tree Analysis

The attack tree analysis is used by attackers when formulating an attack. It is in the form of a flow chart that helps to outline how the attack will be carried out. Security teams usually use the attack tree when performing some risk analysis that is critical. To improve your hacking skills, you should make sure that you are able to plan an attack and also handle it in a methodological manner.

The main challenge that is present is the time that is needed when formulating the attack tree. Also, you should possess the necessary expertise when formulating the attack tree. Nowadays, there are some tools that can be used to formulate the attack tree. You can use the SecurITree tool to formulate the attack tree.

The ethical hacking process is also advancing as compared to the assessment of the present vulnerabilities. As an ethical hacker, you should make sure that you possess a lot of knowledge about varying systems. For example, you can start by looking for some information about the target. Also, you can use varying ethical hacking techniques. At times, you may be undecided and that means that you should assess the system thoroughly to make sure that there is enough visibility. You can also focus more on the firewall.

Formulating the Testing Standards

In an instance whereby there is some form of miscommunication, the system can crash easily when the ethical hacking process is taking place. Make sure that you have come up with testing standards so that you may avoid some challenges. Some of the standards include:

1. When are you performing the tests? Is there a specific time?
2. Which tests are being performed?
3. How will you perform each test and which IP address will you use?
4. The specific amount of knowledge that you possess about the systems that you are going to test.
5. Which are the best steps to take after you have discovered that there are some vulnerabilities within the system.

Some of the practices that you should utilize during the ethical hacking process include:

Timing

The timing is very important and it should also apply during the ethical hacking process. When you carry out some tests, you must make sure that the business process that are going on within the organization are not affected in any way. There are harmful situations that you should also avoid through all means possible including miscommunication. The DoS (Denial of Service) attacks should also be avoided, especially when dealing with an e-commerce site that has high traffic. If there are many people who are involved in handling the project, it is best to agree on the timing so that the end goals can be easily achieved.

It is good to make sure that the ISP (Internet Service Provider) is knowledgeable about the ethical hacking attack that is about to take place. After making sure that they are aware, you can go ahead and assess the vulnerabilities that are present within the system and the ISP (Internet Service Provider) will not try to block the traffic after suspecting that there is some malicious behavior that is taking place.

Make sure that the testing timeline is made up of short-term dates and the tests should be carried out at intervals. Make sure that the milestones are also outlined. The timelines and all the data should be keyed into a spreadsheet so that it can also offer some guidance.

Specific Tests

As an ethical hacker, your services may be required at some point, especially when carrying out penetration tests. Some of the tests include cracking the passwords so that you may be able to gain access to some of the web applications. In some instances, you may need to collect some information that will come in handy when facilitating the attack and that means that you should carry out a social engineering attack. You may need to carry different tests and you should make sure that you have not revealed any information about the tests that you are about to carry out. The documentation process is important since it will help to get rid of the miscommunication that may come about in the future. In some instances, you may have to make sure that you collect some evidence through the use of screenshots. Also, you may lack the knowledge to handle some tests, but that does not mean that the tests cannot take place. In such an instance, you should use the automated tools since you may also be unable to learn more about some of the tests that you should conduct.

About the Blind and Knowledge Assessments

During the testing phase, make sure that you possess enough knowledge about the system and the network. The possession of such knowledge may not be necessary; nevertheless, you should make sure that you possess some basic knowledge about the system that you are about to test and you will also be able to protect yourself by ensuring that there are no digital footprints that can be used to trace back to the individual who facilitated the attack. When you want to learn more about a specific organization, the process is not tough in any way. You just need to carry out a survey as a formality so that you can understand how the system operates and you can go ahead and plan the attack. After carrying out some background research, you will not carry out the attack blindly. When you carry out an assessment, some of the techniques that you have used will depend on the specific needs that you possess.

The best approach that you can use during the hacking process is to make sure that you have come up with a plan that will come in handy when facilitating multiple attacks. Also, as a client, you should make sure that the hacker that you have hired does not harbor any malicious motives. Some of the hackers may have a limited scope depending on the end result that they expect. Also, ensure that the network administrators cannot detect that there is a test that is being carried out. As an attacker, to avoid being caught, you may use social engineering attacks. If a system is being accessed by many people, when they discover that there is an attack taking place, they may change their habits and that means that the expected results will not be accurate. If you want to inform people about the attack, make sure that only the key players such as the IT experts can get a hold of such information.

Location

The tests that you are carrying out as an ethical hacker should dictate the location of where you will carry out the ethical hacking process. The major goal is to make sure that the system has been tested at a location that can be easily accessed by malicious users. The major challenges, in this case, include being unable to determine whether there is someone within the organization who has hacked into the system; as a result, always make sure that all the present loopholes have been sealed. Also, you may combine different tests and they can also be executed both externally and internally.

You can carry out different tests, including cracking the passwords and also assessing the network within the target organization. In some instances, you should also seek the services of another professional who has knowledge about how to hack into a system. Some of the gadgets that you can also test include routers, firewalls, web applications, and servers. When carrying out an external attack, make sure that your internet connection is stable. You may also have to use the external proxy servers. Make sure that you have assigned a specific IP address to the computer that will be used during the vulnerability assessment process. Also, ensure that you have accessed the network outside the firewall. The internal tests are easy and you will only need to have access to the network physically as well as the organization's servers. In some instances, you can also use a cable modem.

How to Handle the Vulnerabilities in the Network

When it comes to handling the vulnerabilities that are within the network, you should make sure that you have come up with sensible techniques that you can use to seal all the loopholes that are within the organization. The hacking process cannot take place forever since the system will be at the risk of crashing. Ensure that you have followed a certain path until you will no longer be able to access the system. You may have some doubts and, in such cases, make sure that you have referred to the goals that you had outlined before you started the ethical hacking process. After discovering some loopholes, make sure that you have contacted the right personnel so that they can also handle the problem fast. If some of these problems are not fixed on a timely basis, some of the external attackers may take advantage of these loopholes and they can also cause some damage that is irreversible. The staff within the company should also make sure that they have not violated any of the employment arrangements within the company.

Silly Assumptions

When you start to assume things, there is a high likelihood that you will not be able to achieve your objectives. There are many assumptions that people make when they are about to hack into a system and they include:

1. You may assume that the networks are available during the testing phase.
2. You may assume that you know all the risks that are present
3. You may also assume that you have all the tools that you need during the testing phase.
4. You may also assume that some of these tools will also minimize the chances of the network crashing.

Make sure that you have documented all the assumptions that you may be having before the ethical hacking process commences.

How to Select the Tools that You Will Use to Carry Out the Vulnerability Assessment

There are some factors that you should consider before you can choose the security assessment tools that you will use during the vulnerability assessment process. For starters, you must consider the tests that you are supposed to run. The ethical hacking tests can also be conducted using a network. When you perform the tests comprehensively, ensure that you have selected the tools appropriately.

Make sure that you have an in-depth understanding of all the tools that you are going to use when scanning for the vulnerabilities. The tools are accompanied by a manual which may be in the form of a Readme file. Make sure that you have opened the file so that you can learn more about how the tools operate and how they should be installed. There are message boards that can also help you to learn more about the tools that are offered by Kali Linux.

Some tools are quite hazardous since they can also affect the health of the network. Make sure that you are very careful when using some of these tools. Also, ensure you have in-depth knowledge about the options that are available. During the ethical hacking phase, do not try to use any tools that you are not conversant with since you may end up causing more harm than good. For instance, you may initiate a DoS (Denial of Service) attack abruptly. Some data may also be lost in the process. If some of the tools that are available for free do not prove to be worth it, you can purchase the commercial versions of the tools since they will be more effective. The main point to note is that some of these commercial tools are quite expensive, but their functionality is superb. Commercial tools ensure that you have gotten value for your money.

6. Kali Linux Tools

In this section, we will go through the different types of tools that are available in Kali Linux. The tools can be classified as per the tasks that are achieved by using them. The classification is as follows:

- Exploitation Tools

- Forensics Tools

- Information Gathering Tools

- Reverse Engineering Tools

- Wireless Attack Tools

- Reporting Tools

- Stress Testing Tools

- Maintaining Access Tools

- Sniffing and Spoofing Tools

- Password Attack Tools

Let us now go through the tools available in each category one by one to understand their specific purpose.

Exploitation Tools

If you consider a network over the Internet, which has a set of computers running on it, there are many applications in each system that can make that system vulnerable. This can happen due to many reasons such as bad code, open ports on the servers, etc., which make these systems easily accessible. This is where exploitation tools come into the picture. They help you target and exploit such vulnerable machines. But you are not an attacker, and therefore, these tools will help you identify and patch these vulnerabilities. Let us go through the available exploitation tools in Kali Linux one at a time.

Armitage
Developed by Raphael Mudge, Armitage is a graphical user interface front-end, which is to be used with the Metasploit framework. It is a tool that is available in the graphical form, and it is easy to use as it recommends exploits on a given system. The tool is open-source and

free to use. It is mostly popular for the data it can provide about shared sessions and the communication it provides through a single instance of Metasploit. A user can launch scans and exploits on a system using Armitage, which will give the user data about available exploits. This, combined with the advanced tools available in the Metasploit framework, gives a user control over a vulnerable system.

The Backdoor Factory (BDF)

The Backdoor Factory known as BDF is a Kali Linux tool that is used by researchers and security professionals. Using this tool, a user can slide in their desired code in the executable binaries of system files on application files. The tool executes the code without letting the system know that there is something additional happening along with the regular system or application processes.

The Browser Exploitation Framework (BeEF)

As the name suggests, if you want to perform penetration testing on browsers, the Browser Exploitation Framework should be your go-to tool. Using this tool, you can also target a browser on the client-side if there are vulnerabilities present in it.

Commix

Commix is a Kali Linux tool which allows users to test web applications. It has been very useful to set up test environments for web developers, penetration testers, and researchers. It performs injections into a web application and allows a user to identify bugs and errors. The tool has been developed in Python.

Crackle

The Crackle tool is a Kali Linux tool, which is used as a brute force utility. It can detect and intercept traffic between Bluetooth devices. The pairing code used between Bluetooth devices is mostly 4-6 digits and is in an encrypted format. Crackle can decrypt these codes, and you can then intercept all communication that happens between the Bluetooth devices.

JBoss-Autopwn

JBoss-Autopwn is a penetration-testing tool used in JBoss applications. The Github version of JBoss Autopwn is outdated, and the last update is from 2011. It is a historical tool and not used much now.

Linux Exploit Suggester

The Linux Exploit Suggester tool provides a script that keeps track of vulnerabilities and shows all possible exploits that help a user get root access during a penetration test.

The script uses the uname -r command to find the kernel version of the Linux operating system. Additionally, it will also provide the -k parameter through which the user can manually enter the version for the kernel of the Linux operating system.

sqlmap
The sqlmap Kali tool is a free and open-source tool that is used for penetration testing. Using this tool, you can detect vulnerabilities in SQL databases and therefore, perform SQL injections. The detection engine on this tool is extremely powerful, and it has a range of tools that can perform extreme penetration allowing a user to fetch information such as data from databases, database fingerprinting, etc. It can also give the user access to the file system in the operating system, thereby allowing the user to execute commands.

Yersinia
The Yersinia tool available in Kali Linux can be used to detect vulnerabilities in network protocols such that a user can take advantage of them. The framework of this tool is solid for testing and analyzing deployment of

systems and networks. The attacks using this tool are layer-2 attacks that can be used to exploit the weaknesses in a layer-2 network protocol. Yersinia is used during penetration tests to start attacks on network devices such as DHCP servers, switches, etc. which use the spanning tree protocol.

Cisco Global Exploiter

The Cisco Global Exploiter (CGE) tool is a security testing exploit engine/tool that is simple yet fast and advanced. There are 14 vulnerabilities that are known to exist in Cisco routers and switches. This tool can be used to exploit those vulnerabilities. The Cisco Global Exploiter is basically a perl script, which is driven using the command line and has a front-end that is simple and easy to use.

Forensics Tools

In this section, we will go through the Kali Linux tools that are available to be used in the Forensics domain.

chkrootkit

The chkrootkit tool can be used during a live boot of a system. It helps identify if there are any rootkits that are installed on the system. The tool helps in hardening the system and lets a user ensure that it is not vulnerable to a hacker. The tool can also be used to perform a system binary scan which lets a user know if there are any modifications made to the stock rootkit, string replacements, temporary deletions, etc. These are just a few of the things that this little tool can do. It looks like a fairly simple tool, but the power it possesses can be invaluable to a forensic investigator.

pOf

The pOf tool is used when you want to know the operating system if a host that is being targeted. You can do this just by intercepting transmitted packages and analyzing them. It does not matter if the system has a firewall or not, the tool will still fetch you the information on the operating system. The tool is amazing as it does not lead to any extra traffic on the network, and its probes are not mysterious at all. Given all these features, pOf in the hands of an advanced user can help detect the presence of firewalls, use of NAT devices, and the presence of load balancers as well.

pdf-parser

The pdf-parser tool can be used to parse a PDF file and identify all the elements used in the file. The output of the tool on a PDF file is not a PDF file. It is not advisable for textbook cases of PDF files, but it gets the job done. The use case of this tool is mostly to identify PDF files that may have scripts embedded into them.

Dumpzilla

The Dumpzilla tool is developed in Python. This tool extracts all information that may be of interest to forensics from web browsers like Seamonkey, Mozilla Firefox, and Iceweasel.

ddrescue

The ddrescue tool is often termed as a savior tool. It is used to copy data from one-block devices such as a hard disk drive to another block device. It is, however, called a savior because while copying data, it will copy all the good parts first, which helps to prevent read errors on the source block device.

The ddrescue tool's basic operation is completely automatic which means that once you have started it, you do not need to wait for any prompts like an error, wherein you would need to stop the program or restart it.

By using the mapfule feature of the tool, data will be recovered in an efficient fashion, as it will only read the blocks that are required. You also have the option to stop the ddrescue process at any time and resume it again later from the same point.

Foremost

There are times when you may have deleted files on purpose or by mistake and realized that you needed them later. The Foremost tool is there to rescue you. This tool is an open-source tool that can be used to retrieve data off of disks that have been completely formatted. The metadata around the file may be lost, but the data retrieved will be intact. A magical feature is that even if the directory information is lost, it can help retrieve data by reference to the header or footer of the file, making it a fast and reliable tool for data recovery.

An interesting fact is that Foremost was developed by special agents of the US Air Force.

Galleta

The Galleta tool helps you parse a cookie trail that you have been following and convert it into a spreadsheet format, which can be exported for future reference.

Whenever a cybercrime case is ongoing, cookies can be used as evidence. But understanding cookies in their raw format is a challenging task. This is where the Galleta tool comes handy as it helps in structuring the data fetched from cookie trails and can be then run through other software to decode the data further. This software needs the input of the date to be in a spreadsheet format, and that is exactly what Galleta feeds into this software.

Information Gathering Tools

The prerequisite for any attack is information. It becomes very easy to target a system when you have sufficient information about the system. The success rate of the attack is also on the higher side when you know everything about the target system. All kinds of information are useful to a hacker, and nothing can be considered as irrelevant.

The process of information gathering includes:

- Gathering information that will help in social engineering and, ultimately, in the attack

- Understanding the range of the network and computers that will be the targets of the attack

- Identifying and understanding all the complete surface of the attack, i.e., processes, and systems that are exposed

- Identifying the services of a system that are exposed and collecting as much information about them as possible

- Querying specific service that will help fetch useful data such as usernames

We will now go through Information Gathering tools available in Kali Linux one by one.

Nmap and Zenmap

Ethical hacking is a phase in Kali Linux for which the tools NMap and ZenMap are used. NMap and ZenMap are basically the same tools. ZenMap is a Graphical Interface for the NMap tool that works on the command line.

The NMap tool, which is used for security auditing and discovery of network, is a free tool. Apart from penetration testers, it is also used by system administrators and network administrators for daily tasks such as monitoring the uptime of the server or a service and managing schedules for service upgrades.

NMap identifies available hosts on a network by using IP packets that are raw. This also helps NMap identify the service being hosted on the host, which includes the name of the application and the version. Basically, the most important application it helps identify on a network is the filter or the firewall set up on a host.

Stealth Scan

The Stealth Scan is also popularly known as the half-open scan or SYN. It is called so because it refrains from completing the usual three-way handshake of TCP. A SYN packet is sent by an attacker to the target host, who then acknowledges the SYN and sends a SYN/ACK in return. If a SYN/ACK is received, it can be safely assumed that the connection to the target host will complete and the port is open and can listen to the target host. If the response received is RST instead, it is safe to assume that the port is closed or not active on the target host.

braa

braa is a tool that is used for scanning mass Simple Network Management Protocol (SNMP). The tool lets you make SNMP queries, but unlike other tools that make single queries at a time to the SNMP service, braa has the capability to make queries to multiple hosts simultaneously, using one single process. The advantage of braa is that it scans multiple hosts very fast and that too by using very limited system resources.

Unlike other SNMP tools that require libraries from SNMP to function, braa implements and maintains its own stack of SNMP. The implementation is very complex and dirty. Supports limited data types, and cannot be called up to standard in any case. However, braa was developed to be a fast tool, and it is fast indeed.

dnsmap

dnsmap is a tool that came into existence originally in 2006 after being inspired by the fictional story "The Thief No One Saw" by Paul Craig.

A tool used by penetration testers in the information gathering stage, dnsmap helps discover the IP of the target company, domain names, netblocks, phone numbers, etc.

Dnsmap also helps on subdomain brute force, which helps in cases where zone transfers of DNS do not work. Zone transfers are not allowed publicly anymore nowadays, which makes dnsmap essential.

Fierce
Fierce is a Kali tool that is used to scan ports and map networks. Discovery of hostnames across multiple networks and scanning of IP spaces that are non-contiguous can be achieved by using Fierce. It is a tool much like Nmap, but in the case of Fierce, it is used specifically for networks within a corporation.

Once the target network has been defined by a penetration tester, Fierce runs a whole lot of tests on the domains in the target network and retrieves information that is valuable and which can be analyzed and exploited by the attacker.

Fierce has the following features.

- Capabilities for a brute-force attack through custom and built-in test list

- Discovery of name servers

- Zone transfer attacks

- Scan through IP ranges both internal and external

- Ability to modify the DNS server for reverse host lookups

Wireshark

Wireshark is a Kali tool that is an open-source analyzer for network and works on multiple platforms such as Linux, BSD, OS X, and Windows.

It helps one understand the functioning of a network, thus making it of use in government infrastructure, education industries, and other corporates.

It is similar to the tcpdump tool, but Wireshark is a notch above as it has a graphical interface through which you can filter and organize the data that has been captured, which means that it takes less time to analyze the data further. There is also an only text-based version known as tshark, which has almost the same amount of features.

Wireshark has the following features.

- The interface has a user-friendly GUI

- Live capture of packets and offline analysis

- Support for Gzip compression and extraction

- Inspection of the full protocol

- Complete VoIP analysis

- Supports decryption for IPsec, Kerberos, SSL/TLS, WPA/WPA2

URLCrazy

URLCrazy is a Kali tool that tests and generates typos and variations in domains to target and perform URL hijacking, typo squatting, and corporate espionage. It has a database that can generate variants of up to 15 types for domains and misspellings of up to 8000 common spellings. URLCrazy supports a variety of keyboard layouts, checks if a particular domain is in use and figures how popular a typo is.

Metagoofil

Metagoofil is a Kali tool that is aimed at retrieving files such as pdf, xls, doc, ppt, etc.which are publicly available for a company on the Internet. The tool makes a Google search to scan the Internet and download such files to the local machine. The tool then extracts the metadata of these files using libraries such as pdfminer, hachoir, etc. The output from this tool is then fed as input to the information-gathering pipeline. The inputs include usernames, server or machine names, and software version, which help penetration testers with their investigation.

Ghost Phisher

Ghost Phisher is a Kali tool, which is used as an attack software program and also for security auditing of wired and wireless networks. Ghost Phisher is developed in the Python programming language. The program basically emulates access points of a network, therefore, deploying its own internal server into a network.

Fragroute

Traffic moving towards a specific system can be intercepted and modified with the use of the Fragroute tool in Kali Linux. In simple words, the packets originating from the attacker system known as frag route packets are routed strategically to a destination system. Attackers and security personnel use it to bypass firewalls. Information gathering is a use case for fragroute and is therefore widely used by attackers or penetration testers.

Reverse Engineering Tools

We can learn how to make and break things from something as simple as a Lego toy to a car engine simply by dismantling the parts one by one and then putting them back together. This process wherein we break things down to study it deeply and further improve it is called Reverse Engineering.

The technique of Reverse Engineering in its initial days would only be used with hardware. As the process evolved over the years, engineers started applying it to software, and now to human DNA as well. Reverse engineering, in the domain of cyber security, helps understand that if a system was breached, how the attacker entered the system and the steps that he took to break and enter into the system.

While getting into the network of corporate infrastructure, attackers ensure that they are utilizing all the tools available to them in the domain of computer intrusion tools. Most of the attackers are funded and skilled and have a specific objective for an attack towards which they are highly motivated. Reverse Engineering empowers us to put up a fight against such attackers in the future. Kali Linux comes equipped with a lot of tools that are useful in the process of reverse engineering in the digital world. We will list down some of these tools and learn their use.

Apktool

Apktool is a Kali Linux tool that is used in the process of reverse engineering. This tool has the ability to break down resources to a form that is almost the original form and then recreate the resource by making adjustments. It can also debug code that is small in size, step by step. It has a file structure, which is project-like, thus making it easy to work with an app. With Apktool, you can also automate tasks that are repetitive in nature, like the building of an apk.

Dex2jar

Dex2jar is a Kali tool, which has a lightweight API and was developed to work with the Dalvik Executable that is the .dex/.odex file formats. The tool basically helps to work with the .class files of Java and Android.

It has the following components.

- Dex2jar has an API that is lightweight, similar to that of ASM.

- dex-translator component does the action of converting a job. It reads instructions from dex to the dex-ir format and converts it to ASM format after optimizing it.

- Dex-ir component, which is used by the dex-translator component, basically represents the dex instructions.

- The dex-tools component works with the .class files. It is used for tasks such as modifying an apk, etc.

diStorm3

diStorm is a Kali tool which is easy to use the decomposer library and is lightweight at the same time. Instructions can be disassembled in 16 bit, 32 bit and 64-bit modes using diStorm. It is also popular amongst penetration testers as it is the fast disassembler library. The source code, which depends on the C library, is very clean, portable, readable, and independent of a particular platform, which allows it to be used in embedded modules and kernel modules.

diStorm3 is the latest version which is backward compatible with diStorm64's old interface. However, using the new header files is essential.

edb-debugger

edb debugger is a Kali tool which is the Linux equivalent for the popular Windows tool called "Olly debugger." It is a debugging tool with modularity as one of its main goals. Some of its features are as follows.

- An intuitive Graphical User Interface

- All the regular debugging operations such as step-into, step-over, run and break

- Breakpoints for conditions

- Basic analysis for instructions

- View or Dump memory regions

- Address inspection which is effective

- Generation and import of symbol maps

- Various available plugins

The core that is used for debugging is integrated as a plugin so that it can be replaced when needed as per requirement.

The view of the data dump is in tabbed format. This feature allows the user to open several views of the memory at a given time while allowing you to switch between them.

Jad Debugger

Jad is a Kali Linux tool that is a Java decompiler and the most popular one in the world. It is a tool which runs on the command line and is written in the C++ language. Over the years, there have been many graphical interfaces which have been developed which run Jad in the background and provide a comfortable front end to the users to perform tasks such as project management, source browsing, etc. Kali Linux powers Jad in its releases to be used for Java application debugging and other processes of reverse engineering.

JavaSnoop

JavaSnoop is a Kali Linux tool that allows testing of Java application security. By developing JavaSnoop, Aspect has proved how it's a leader in the security industry in providing verification services for all applications and not just web-based applications.

JavaSnoop allows you to begin tampering with method calls, run customized code, or sit back and see what's going on the system by just attaching an existing process such as a debugger.

OllyDbg

OllyDbg is a Kali Linux tool which is a debugger at a level of a 32-bit Assembler developed for Microsoft Windows. What makes it particularly useful is its emphasis on code that is in binary in times when the source is not available.

OllyDbg brags of the following features.

- Has an interactive user interface and no command-line hassle

- Loads and debugs DLLs directly

- Allows function descriptions, comments and labels to be defined by the user

- No trash files in the registry or system directories post installation

- Can be used to debug multi-threaded applications

- Many third-party applications can be integrated as it has an open architecture

- Attaches itself to running programs

Valgrind

Valgrind is a tool in Kali Linux tool which is used for profiling and debugging Linux based systems. The tool allows you to manage threading bugs and memory management bugs automatically. It helps eliminate hours that one would waste on hunting down bugs and therefore, stabilizes the program to a very great extent. A program's processing speed can be increased by doing detailed profiling on the program by using Valgrind too. Suite for debugging and profiling Linux programs. The Valgrind distribution has the following production-quality tools currently.

- Memcheck which detects errors in memory

- DRD and Helgrind which are two other thread error detectors

- Cachegrind is a branch prediction and cache profiling tool

- Callgrind is a branch detection profile and a call-graph generating cache profiler

- Massif which profiles heaps

- Three experimental tools are also included in the Valgrind distribution.

- SGCheck which detector for stack or global array overrun

- DHAT which is a second profiler for heap and helps understand how heap blocks are being used

- BBV which basic block vector generator

Reverse Engineering plays an important role where manufacturers are using it to sustain competition from rivals. Other times reverse engineering is used to basically figure out flaws in software and re-build a better version of the software. Kali Linux provides tools which are known in the reverse engineering domain. In addition to the tools that we have discussed, there are many 3rd party reverse engineering tools as well but the ones we have discussed come installed in the Kali Linux image.

7. Malware And Cyber Attacks

In this chapter, we start talking about *malware types*, and later on we will discuss *Cyber Attacks*. For starters, we will discuss Viruses, Trojans, Worms, Ransomware and other types of programs that were badly designed. But first of all, let us answer the following question:

1) What is a Malware ?

A *malware* (aka. malicious software) is a malicious software program designed to steal, destroy, or corrupt data stored on our devices.

Many people use the *generic term of the virus*, which is not necessarily correct because there can be many types of dangerous programs. Here below (only) a part of them:

1) *Virus*
2) *Trojans*
3) *Worms*
4) *Ransomware*
5) *Spyware*
6) *Adware*

7) and many more (Rootkit, time bombs, backdoor, etc.)

Here is the picture below on **Wikipedia**, the proportion (in 2011) of malware from the Internet. Since then, many things have changed or changed, but it's interesting to have such a hierarchy with the most common types of malware.

And now take some of these malware and discuss them in more detail:

1) Viruses

A virus is a program with which we are all accustomed to. Whether we had the computer infected with a virus or that we heard / seen someone else, we know that these viruses can be really dangerous for us (and especially for our data stored on the computer - the most important element for us).

Virus programmers take advantage of existing vulnerabilities in different operating systems (especially Windows) and write software to take advantage of them (and users of these devices).

2) Trojans

A Trojan is a type of program designed to appear for the benefit of the person who uses it, but there is a malicious code behind that has other intentions altogether. These types of programs are most common in the Internet (as you could see in the picture above) and are used to being easily masked in front of an inexperienced user. So in the (first) run of the program, the trojan is installed and will hide, doing its job "quietly". The term Trojan comes from the story of the Trojan horse in Greek mythology, exposed in the movie Troy.

3) Worms

A worm is a form of malware that once it infects a device (PC, laptop, server, etc.) will do its best to expand and infect others on the network. Thus, a worm manages to *slow networks* and the connected devices (by using CPU and RAM resources) and even the network, because infected computers will generate abnormal traffic.

4) Ransomware

A more popular type of malware lately is ransomware, whose purpose is to *encrypt the hard disk* (or SSD) victims and to request a cash *redeem* for the decryption key.

5) Adware

There are programs that once installed on a device (or in the browser) will start to show commercials (annoying).

6) Spyware

Spyware are programs designed to extract certain data from users. They are not meant to hurt (by consuming resources) or affect the victim in any way, but simply extract data and send them to "mother servers" (those who have initiated "espionage").

First, you need to be aware of the existence of such programs, after which you have to take protection / prevention measures against them.

In this situation, anti-virus programs are very welcome because they contain very large databases (called signatures) that check every program / file on your operating system (Windows, Linux or Mac).

Now you can also know that Windows has the highest number of malware (viruses, Trojans, ransomware, etc.). Why? Because Windows is the most widely used operating system in the world, and hackers have something to "steal." That's why the main focus of attackers and cyber-security companies is on Windows.

The Mac and Linux are also not free from malware, but their number is not that big. They have been designed with a higher degree of security in mind and operate completely differently from Windows.

Examples of Cyber Attacks

These hacking methods are very common, and each one serves a particular purpose.

What is a Cyber Attack?

A cyber attack is a means by which a person (with evil intentions) takes advantage of the *vulnerabilities* existing on a particular system (server, computer, network equipment, application, etc.).

Here are some of the most common attacks on the Internet:

1) *MITM-Man in the Middle*

2) *DoS-Denial of Service*

3) *DDoS-Distributed Denial of Service*, check this link: http://www.digitalattackmap.com/

4) *SQLi-SQL* injection

5) *XSS-Cross-Site Scripting*

In addition, there are many more in the Internet world, but to illustrate some, we will only focus on the top 3. So let's take the first type of attack, MITM, and discuss it in more detail about it (and show you some ways you can make such attacks - but please do it in an ethical way), after which will go further with the discussion and discuss DoS and DDoS.

After all, in we will discuss web security and other types of attacks: SQL injections and XSS.

What is a MITM (Man In The Middle) attack ?

MITM is a type of cyber attack in order to listen to the traffic of users connected to the same network.

What this means? It means that if you go to a café in town, someone can connect with you to the same Wi-Fi, and from just a few commands you can see all your conversations on Facebook, Google, etc.

That's how it is, but do not worry because things are not that simple. Why? Because the vast majority of our Internet connections are secured (*HTTPS instead of HTTP*;)), instead it does not mean that there can be no one listening to your traffic.

To avoid such situations, I recommend that you use a VPN in public places.

There are several ways you can do MITM (I will list below just a few of the many possibilities below):

- MAC Spoofing
- ARP Spoofing
- Rogue DHCP Server
- STP Attack
- DNS Poisoning

These are some of the most common. In the following I will discuss some of these and I will give you some practical examples of how to do it.

1) MAC Spoofing

The term spoofing comes from deceiving, and in this case it refers to the deception of at least one device in the network by the fact that a certain computer is given as another computer (or even Router) using its MAC address.

This can be done very easily using a program that changes your MAC address with a PC to see its traffic. Here's an example (https://windowsreport.com/mac-address-changer-windows-10/) on Windows 10 about how to change your MAC address, but in my opinion the process is much more complex, compared to Linux:

ifconfig eth0 down

macchanger -m *00:d0:70:00:20:69 eth0*

ifconfig eth0 up

First, we stop the interface (eth0 in this example), then we use the *macchanger* command that helps us with

the *MAC address change*, and the -m argument lets us specify an address. For verification, use the command:
#ifconfig

PS: If you want to *generate a random MAC*, then use:
#macchanger -r eth0

2) ARP Spoofing
ARP Spoofing works in a similar way to MAC spoofing, just as the attacker uses the ARP protocol to mislead the entire network about having the MAC address X (which is actually the Router). Thus, all network devices that want to reach the Internet will send the traffic to the attacker (which will redirect it to Router). In this situation, the attacker can see all the traffic passing through him using a traffic capture program such as Wireshark.

To initiate such an attack first we must *start the routing process on Linux* so that traffic can be sent from the victim to the Router and vice versa (through us, the "attackers"):

 # echo "1" > proc/sys/net/ipv4/ip_forward
 # cat /proc/sys/net/ipv4/ip_forward
Now we are *redirecting* the traffic to the port we want to listen to:

iptables -t nat -A PREROUTING -p tcp --destination-port 80 -j REDIRECT --to-port 8181

After which we need to install the program:

sudo apt-get update

sudo apt-get install *dsniff*

And now we can give the command to start the attack:

sudo arpspoof -i *eth0* -t *192.168.1.3 192.168.1.1*

sudo arpspoof -i *eth0* -t *192.168.1.1 192.168.1.3*

- -i eth0: is the interface on which we will start the attack

- -t 192.168.1.3: is the IP of the victim (the device we want to attack - CHANGE with an IP from your network)

- 192.168.1.1: is the Router IP (CHANGE the Router IP to your Router)

Virtually these two orders, send fake packages to the two devices informing them that traffic has to pass through the attacker. Now all you have to do is open Wireshark and see how the victim's traffic "passes through you".

Here is another need for an element that will facilitate the *DECRYPTION of traffic*. Why? Because much of the Internet traffic is encrypted.

With this tool we will use: *SSLstrip* (removes the security element, SSL), and the command to decrypt HTTPS traffic in HTTP is:

sudo python *sslstrip.py -l 8181*

This command will listen to traffic on port 8181 and try to decrypt it. After that, you can start Wireshark and see the encrypted traffic (however, I suggest you start Wireshark and when the traffic is encrypted to see the difference).

PS: At a simple search on Google you will find SSLstrip;)

To write the result to a file (from the terminal) you can use a tool similar to Wireshark called *Ettercap*. Once you install it on Linux you can give the following command:

*sudo* **ettercap −i eth0 −T −w /root/scan.txt −M**
   arp /192.168.1.3 /

The arguments used in the command are:

- -i eth0: the interface on which traffic is listened

- -T : to launch command execution over the terminal

- -M : Man in middle mode

- -w : writing data to a file

- 192.168.1.3: the victim's IP address

8. Virtual Private Networks To Help

The next thing that we need to take a look at is the Virtual Private Network. The VPN is going to be a means of extending a local network to the external nodes so that these nodes are going to become a part of the local network. This practice is going to have a lot of legitimate uses, including allowing the network of a corporate in disparate geographical areas to help them connect and share resources in a secure manner. Of course, it would also provide hackers with a big advantage so that they can join in with a network of a target server if they know how to work with this network in the right manner.

VPN's and Tunneling
The power of a VPN is going to lie in a practice that is known as tunneling. Instead of connecting to a destination server through the internet via a service provider, the user is going to establish an encrypted connection to the VPN server, which is then going to help get them connected with their destination. Although the ISP is able to see whether the user is connected to a known VPN server IP address, it is not

able to read through all of the encrypted traffic that happens here either.

When a request is sent from the user over to the server of the VPN, then the VPN is going to decrypt the request (which is going to include the headers for the destination), and then it will relay it through the internet. When packets are sent back to the VPN, this will be encrypted again and relayed back to the user with the right tunnel that has already been established.

VPN Types and Uses

The next thing that we need to take a look at here is the VPN types and uses. They are going to be two main options that we can work with on this server and they are going to be categorized based on their purpose. This includes the site-to-site options and remote access. The remote access VPN is going to be the one that is the most commonly used by home or personal users to either protect their anonymity or to make sure that they can bypass some restrictions such as regional access, corporate access, or ISP access.

Home or corporate users could potentially use this kind of VPN if they would like to reach their own LANs from a location that is outside the office. This arrangement could be the most desirable with a company that has personnel that works remotely or when there are multiple locations, but they still need to have a central access place for their services and databases. Home users have the option of setting up one of these VPN in a manner that is similar here in order to access their files at their own home or to allow them a way to have control over their own computer from a remote location.

Although having that access to a VPN remotely can create a connection that is encrypted, it is going to be done through a process of encapsulating packets that are traveling through the internet in a manner that looks just like the standard traffic. The site-to-site VPNs are going to help us create a more secure connection by employing any protocol that can maintain the communication that happens between the routers. This communication is only something that is possible when the server and the client come together and mutually authenticate the information.

VPN Protocols
The type of protocol that your VPN is going to use depends largely on what the purpose of your server will be, and some of the needs of your user. Many

commercial VPN services are going to be helpful in allowing the clients to select the protocol of the server that they would like to work with. This choice is often going to be seen as a type of trade-off that can happen between speed, reliability, and security.

Encryption, by its very nature, is going to slow down the connection speeds a little bit in order to hide the message but since there is often more than one user that us sharing that server access, heavy congestion is going to be a much more likely cause of the slower speeds. The type of content that you want to access can affect the choice is protocol as well. For example, audio streaming and video streaming are going to require the UDP port support and more bandwidth than just what we see with regular HTTP browsing, so we have to consider the speed of that as well.

Now there are a few different protocols that we are able to choose when it comes to the VPN that we want to use and how we want to make sure that it is protected. The first option is going to be an open VPN. This is a very common and popular protocol for VPN that is going to use a lot of different libraries, which are all open-sourced, to help with communication and encryption.

The biggest advantage that we are able to see with this kind of protocol is that it can easily be applied to any port or sub-layer protocol that you want to work with, especially when we are talking about security. One of the drawbacks is that most browsers that are out there right now are not able to support this natively and you will need to rely on some third-party software to make sure that your mobile device or computer is able to connect to this server if you would like to use this protocol.

The next type of VPN protocol that we are able to work with is known as the point-to-point tunneling protocol or PPTP. This is an older protocol, but there are still many programmers who use it. The PPTP is going to offer us some encryption, but it is replete with a lot of security vulnerabilities and because of its age, it is possible that it is going to be exploited more than some of the others.

However, because it is able to support some of the older platforms as well as some of the legacy operating systems, and because it is still easy to use, this is a protocol that, despite the drawbacks, is commonly found. Many of the VPN services are going to provide this PPTP as an option for their clients who like to use it or will need it, but they also take the time to warn the clients about some of the security risks as well.

And the third option that we are able to work with is known as Layer 2 Tunneling Protocol or L2TP. This is one of the protocols that can be chosen because it is easy to use and the native support, but the channel that you are relying on is not going to be all that secure. In fact, this protocol is not going to be able to perform some of its own data encryption, so we will need to combine it together with a few other encryption protocols to get the work done. Another drawback that we may see with this option is that it has to be confined to just one port, which is going to make it easier for an ISP or firewall to block, and not that great for the hacker to work with.

Choosing Our VPN
A home user is going to look to use this kind of VPN, and whatever protocol they decide to go with, for anonymity, security, and freedom when it is time to connect to the internet. And often they are going to come with a few choices, with some trade-offs occurring between the speed, reliability, security, and cost.

Although the VPNs provide encryption, and an exit node for clients to hide their identity quite a bit, as a hacker, you want to make sure that you know whether or not someone is able to log or track your activities.

One of the things that we need to take a look at when choosing one of these VPNs is whether user logging is going on. If the VPN activity logs are either being subpoenaed by law enforcement or compromised by hackers, then the relative anonymity that is provided by the exit node is no longer going to be the advantage. If the user would like to add in that layer of anonymity, then they need to make sure that the VPN that they go with is a no-logging service. Though keep in mind that no logging really means minimal logging.

There is going to be a certain amount of internal logging that will occur in order to make sure that the VPN is able to maintain their connection reliability and speed and to make sure that there aren't any attacks on the servers. The best services are going to work with just the minimum amount of logging that is necessary to help keep up a stable operation, and they will not keep records of those logs for any longer than they need.

As a hacker here, we need to make sure that we are skeptical of a VPN, especially one that claims to be free when they state that they do not log any activity, at least until you can read the fine print and find out exactly what the company does and does not log. In addition, these free services are not necessarily going to be that trustworthy on their own. Using your own due diligence is a must before you use any free VPN.

Additional Security Considerations with a VPN
If a user is hesitant to purchase a subscription to some of the reputable VPN services because they are worried that all of the anonymity is going to be lost with that transaction, there are a few commercial VPNs out there that will allow you to use something like bitcoin to help pay for it. If you are worried about having your identity revealed through the logs of these systems, even if the server is a no logging server, it is possible to combine together a few VPN connections with a process that is known as VPN chaining.

This is going to be accomplished when we can connect the VPN over to a host machine, then we will set up a different service for VPN on the virtual machine within the same host. If any of the logs are compromised with the inner VPN, the activity is still going to be logged as it came to form the outer VPN. There is the potential that someone would try to get the logs of the outer one, but it is still an additional obstacle and one that most companies and more are not going to take.

Notice here that there are a few VPN services that will provide you with the option of connecting from the VPN server to the destination with the help of the Onion network that we talked about before. Although this is able to provide us with a few extra security advantages, it is also going to come with a reduction in the connection speed so we have to consider that as well.

9. Attacking With Frameworks

Social Engineering

Due to the increase in the use of technology for almost all of our activities, companies and organizations have invested a huge amount of money in ensuring that the technologies they use are properly secured from hackers. These companies have developed and implemented extensive firewalls to protect against any possible security breach. Most internet users are not security conscious despite the ease with which information can be obtained over an internet connection. This is coupled with the fact that most malicious hackers concentrate their efforts on computer servers and client application flaws. Over the years, these hackers have become more creative in how they gather information and structure their attacks on websites and web apps. With the enormous amount of money invested in online security, we would expect that malicious information theft or control would have been eliminated. However, this has not happened.

This is where we use social engineering to achieve our goal. It is a non-technical approach circumvents a company's security measures. No matter how secure a company's online applications are, they are still susceptible to hacking. Hackers have been able to achieve this using social engineering and tools based on social engineering. Social engineering is a hands-on approach to hacking. It involves targeting individuals and manipulating them into giving out vital information that can lead to a breach in the security system. These individuals, who may be employees of the organization or even a close relative of the top person at the target organization, are approached and coerced into trusting the hacker. They begin to gather information that could be of use in the hacking process. This is usually an approach taken when the company's firewalls are effective at thwarting outside penetration. When the hackers have obtained the necessary information (for instance, the login information of the social engineering target), they can hack the company from the inside out.

It is believed that human beings are the weakest link in any information security chain. The physical approach toward social engineering can occur in so many ways that it is impossible to cover all of them in this chapter. However, popular means include approaching and becoming friends with (or even a significant other of) employees at the company. Sometimes the employees are given a flash drive containing movies or other files in which they may be interested. The employees plug in the drive and launch a file that executes scripts in the background, granting the hackers access to the respective machines. The social engineer attack can also occur when a person calls an employee of a firm, impersonates a call center representative and tells the employee that he or she needs information to rectify a service that is important. The hacker would have gathered details about the employee from the employee's social media account or through personal conversations with the person. Once the hacker has received the information (which may include the victim's social security number or login details), the hacker hijacks the account and performs fraudulent transactions on it, or uses it for additional attacks. Social engineering makes it easy to build a username and password list that helps with logging into the target's accounts.

Hackers use the information they have gathered in combination with tools that ensure an easy hack of the company's system. Most of these tools are used in the client-side attack and are enhanced with the information gathered through social engineering. This information is used in conjunction with phishing and spoofing tools to attack a client if a direct social engineering attack fails. Social engineering is the information gathering procedure in this approach when it comes to attacking clients. Hacking has become a business venture. Hackers gain access to information simply to sell it for money, or to use it to transfer money. The motivation now is monetary. Usually, the target is selected, and the hacker uses information available to the public about the client to develop the attack. Typically, information obtained online is sufficient to build an attack. However, with an increase in employee education regarding hackers and social engineering, employees have begun to limit the personal information they share on social media and other public platforms.

The success of a social-engineering-based attack depends solely on the quality of information gathered. The attacker must be sociable and persuasive when interacting with the victim, such that the victim becomes open and begins to trust the hacker. Some hackers outsource this aspect to an individual who is skilled in getting people to tell them secrets.

Social Engineering Toolkit (SET)

The Social Engineering Toolkit is a very important tool used in a computer-aided social engineering attack. It comes pre-installed with the Kali Linux distro. It is written in the Python language and is also an open source toolkit. The Social Engineering Toolkit, or SET, was created by David Kennedy to exploit the human aspect of web security. However, it is important to make sure that the Social Engineering Toolkit is up to date. Once the tool has been updated, the configuration file can be set. The default configuration file is sufficient to make the SET run without any problems. Advanced users may want to edit and tweak certain settings. However, if you are a beginner, it is better to leave it the way it is until you become more familiar with the Social Engineering Toolkit. To access the configuration file, open the terminal and then change the directory to the SET. Open the config folder and you will find the set_config file, which you can open and edit with a text editor to change the parameters.

The Social Engineering Toolkit can be accessed by clicking on the Application icon, then clicking on the Kali Linux desktop. Next, click on BackTrack and then on the Exploitation Tools option. Click on Social Engineering

Tools and select the Social Engineering Toolkit by clicking on SET. The SET will open in a terminal window. Alternatively, the SET can be opened directly from the terminal by typing "setoolkit" without the quotes.

The Social Engineering Toolkit opens in the terminal as a menu-based option. The menu contains different options based on the type of social engineering attack you need to use. The option at number 1 is for spear-phishing vectors which enable the user to execute a phishing attack. The phishing attack is an email attack. It is like casting a net by sending emails to random potential victims. Spear-phishing, on the other hand, targets one individual and the email is more personalized.

The second option on the SET menu is the website attack vector, which uses different web-attack methods against its target victim. The website attack vector option is by far the most popular and perhaps most used option in the Social Engineering Toolkit. Clicking on the website attack vector option opens menus containing the Java applet attack vector, the Metasploit browser exploits, the credential harvester attack used in cloning websites, the tabnabbing attack, the man-in-the-middle attack, the web jacking attack and the multi-attack web method.

The third option on the Social Engineering Toolkit menu is the infectious media generator tool. This is a very easy tool to use and is targeted at individuals who can give a hacker access to the organization network, thus enabling the hacker to hack from inside the network. This tool allows the hacker to create a USB disk or DVD containing a malicious script that gives the hacker access to the target shell. Choosing this option opens a menu with a prompt to choose from between a file-format exploit or a standard Metasploit executable. Choosing the file-format option opens a list of payloads from which to select. The default is a PDF file embedded in an executable script. This is then sent to the drive where the autorun.inf is created with the PDF file. When an employee opens the file on the drive, the file is executed in the background and the hacker gains shell access to the victim's computer.

The fourth option is the generate-a-payload-with-listener option. This option allows the hacker to create a malicious script as a payload and therefore generate a listener. This script is a .exe file. The key is getting the intended victim to click and download this script. Once the victim downloads the .exe file and executes it, the listener alerts the hacker, who can access the victim's shell.

The fifth option in the Social Engineering Toolkit is the mass mailer option. Clicking this option brings up a menu with two options: single email address attack and the mass mailer email attack. The single email address attack allows the user to send an email to a single email address while the mass mailer email attack allows the user to send an email to multiple email addresses. Choosing this option prompts the user to select a list containing multiple email addresses to which the email is then sent.

Sixth on the list is the Arduino-based attack. With this option, you are given the means to compromise Arduino-based devices. The seventh option, on the other hand, is the SMS spoofing option, which enables the hacker to send SMS to a person. This SMS spoofing option opens a menu with an option to perform an SMS spoofing form of attack or create a social-engineering template. Selecting the first option will send to a single number or a mass SMS attack. Selecting just a single number prompts the user to enter the recipient's phone number. Then you are asked to either use a predefined template or craft your own message. Typing 1 chooses the first option while typing 2 chooses the second option depending on your preference for the SMS. Then you enter the source number, which is the number you want the recipient to see as the sender of the SMS. Next, you type the message you want the recipient to see. You can embed links to a phishing site or to a page that will cause the user to download a malicious .exe file. After the message has been crafted, the options for services used in SMS spoofing appear on the screen. Some are paid options and others are free.

Option eight in the SET is the wireless AP attack vector. This option is used to create a fake wireless AP to which unsuspecting users of public Wi-Fi can connect and the hacker can sniff their traffic. This option uses other applications in achieving this goal. AirBase-NG, AirMon-NG, DNSSpoof and dhcpd3 are the required applications that work hand in hand with the wireless AP attack vector.

Option nine in the menu is the QR code attack vector. Today, QR codes are used everywhere, from the identification of items to obtaining more details about products on sale. Now QR codes are even used to make payments. Some websites use QR codes for logins or as web apps. This login method is used because it is perceived as a more secure way of gaining access due to hackers' being able to steal cookies, execute a man-in-the-middle attack and even use a brute-force password to gain unauthorized access. However, this increase in the use of QR codes has given hackers more avenues for exploiting their victims. The QR code attack vector helps the hacker create a malicious QR code. Then the hacker creates or clones a website like Facebook using the credential harvester option and embeds this malicious QR code with the link to the cloned website. The hacker then sends a phishing email or spoofed SMS to a victim, which prompts that person to scan the code with a mobile device. This reveal's the victim's GPS location and other information when the victim visits the website and enters their login details.

The tenth option in the menu is the PowerShell attack vector. This option allows the hacker to deploy payloads in the PowerShell of an operating system. The PowerShell is a more powerful option than the command prompt in the Windows operating system. It allows access to different areas of the operating system. It was developed by Microsoft to ease the automation of tasks and configuration of files and has come with the Windows operating system since the release of Windows Vista. The PowerShell attack vector enables the attacker to create a script that is then executed in the victim's PowerShell. The selection of this option brings out four menu options: PowerShell alphanumeric injector, PowerShell SAM database, PowerShell reverse and PowerShell bind shells. Any of these options creates a targeted PowerShell program and is exported to the PowerShell folder. Tricking the target to access, download and execute this program creates access for the attacker.

By now, you should realize how powerful the SET is in executing computer-aided social engineering attacks. This tool is very valuable for a penetration tester, as it provides a robust and diverse means of checking the various vulnerabilities that may exist in an organization's network.

BeEF

BeEF stands for Browser Exploitation Framework. This tool comes with most of the security-based Linux distro, like the Parrot OS and Kali Linux. BeEF started as a server that was accessed through the attacker's browser. It was created to target vulnerabilities in web browsers that would give access to the target systems for executing commands. BeEF was written in the Ruby language on the Rails platform by a team headed by Wade Alcorn. As stated before, passwords, cookies, login credentials and browsing history are all typically stored on the browser, so a BeEF attack on a client can be very nasty.

On Kali Linux, however, BeEF has been included in the distro. The BeEF framework can be started by going into applications, clicking on exploitation tools and then clicking on the BeEF XSS framework. This brings up a terminal that shows the BeEF framework server has been started. Once the server has been started, we open our browser of choice and visit the localhost at port 3000. This is written in the URL space of the browser as localhost:3000/ui/authentication or 127.0.0.1:3000/ui/authentication. This would bring us to the authentication page of the BeEF framework, requiring a login username and password. By default, the username is beef ; the password is also beef.

Once you are in the BeEF framework, it will open a "Get Started" tab. Here you are introduced to the framework and learn how to use it. Of particular importance is hooking a browser. Hooking a browser involves clicking a JavaScript payload that gives the BeEF framework access to the client's browser. There are various ways by which we can deploy this payload, but the simplest way is to create a page with the payload, prompt the target to visit that page and execute the JavaScript payload. You can be very creative about this aspect. On the other hand, there is a link on the Get Started page that redirects you to The Butcher page. Below this page are buttons containing the JavaScript payload. Clicking on this button will execute the script and, in turn, hook your browser. When your browser is hooked, you will see a hook icon beside your browser icon on the left side of the BeEF control panel with the title "Hooked browser" along with folders for online and offline browsers.

Once a browser is hooked, whether it's online or offline, we can control it from our BeEF control panel. Clicking on the details menu in the control panel will provide information like the victim's browser version and the plugins that are installed. The window size of the browser also can be used to determine the victim's screen size, the browser platform (which is also the operating system on the PC), and a lot more information. For executing commands on the browser, we click on the command menu in the control panel. This brings up a different command we can execute on the victim's browser. This command would create a pop-up message on the victim's browser, so it can be renamed creatively before execution to avoid raising any suspicion. Some of the commands that can be executed in this menu include the Get all Cookie command (which starts harvesting the victim's browser cookies), the Screenshot command, the Webcam command for taking pictures of the victim, the Get visited URL command and so on. There are a lot of commands in this menu.

The BeEF framework JavaScript payload can also hook mobile phone browsers. Checking the details tab after hooking will give that particular information if we end up hooking a phone browser. Clicking on the module and searching the PhoneGap command allows us to execute phone targeted commands like geolocating the device and starting an audio recording on the victim's device. Clicking on the Ipec menu also displays a terminal we can use to send shell commands to the victim's system.

Once the BeEF framework hooks a browser, the possibilities are endless. We can do virtually anything. Therefore, it is important to be careful when clicking links and pop-up or flash messages.

METASPLOIT

The Metasploit framework is perhaps the larget, most complete penetration testing and security auditing tool today. This tool is an open source tool that is regularly updated with new modules for monitoring even the most recent vulnerabilities. Metasploit comes with the Kali Linux distro. It is written in Ruby, although when it was created it was written in Perl. This tool was developed by HD Moore in 2003 and was then sold to an IT company called Rapid7 in 2009.

Metasploit is an immensely powerful tool that has great versatility. To fully utilize Metasploit, you must be comfortable using the terminal, which is a console type window. However, there is an option that allows for the use of Metasploit in a GUI window. Armitage, an opensource tool, makes this possible, although it does not have the capacity to fully utilize all aspects of the

Metasploit framework in an attack. The meterpreter in the Metasploit framework is a module that is dumped in the victim's system, making it easy for the hacker to control that PC and maintain access for future hacks in that system. Getting started with Metasploit on Kali Linux is as good as opening the terminal and typing "msfconsole" without the quotes.

Metasploit contains modules that can be used during a hack. Some of these modules are written by developers or contributors from the open source community. An important set of modules includes the payloads. The payloads are very important when it comes to performing attacks within the Metasploit framework. These payloads are codes that have been written so that the hacker can gain a foothold in the victim's computer. Perhaps the most popular among these payloads is the meterpreter. This particular payload is very powerful, as it leaves no trace of a hack on the system's drive. It exists solely on the victim's system memory.

Then there is the Exploits module. These exploits are codes that have been written and packed for specific flaws in a victim's operating system. Different exploits exist for different operating system flaws, so flaws that are targeted for one vulnerability would fail when used for another.

The encoders are modules that encode the different payloads deployed into the target system to avoid detection by the victim's antivirus, anti-spyware or other security tools.

Other modules available on the Metasploit framework are the Post modules (which allow the hacker to gather passwords, tokens and hashes), the Nops modules (most of which allow for 100 percent execution of the payload or exploit) and the Auxiliary modules (which do not fit into other categories).

This framework is quite robust, as many kinds of hacking procedures can be carried out. Several procedures are executed by combining the modules and making them work in different ways. A good way for a beginner to learn more about the Metasploit framework is to type "help" without the quotes in the Metasploit framework console.

10. Real Examples Of How To Hack With Kali Linux

Kali Linux has more than 600 tools. Each one of these tools performs different functions. Since there are different types of hackers, each hacker will always try to look into the vulnerabilities that are present within the system. The white hat hackers ensure that they have patched all the present vulnerabilities. The black hat hackers usually take advantage of these vulnerabilities so that they can gain access to different pieces of information that they will use for their own personal gain. We will now look into some of the examples on how a person can hack when using Kali Linux.

When carrying out an attack, you must make sure that you have carried out a pilot study. It helps you to gather information that you will use hen launching an attack. After identifying some vulnerabilities, you can exploit a network or even the web applications. During the exploitation process, some of the factors that you should consider include:

- The attacker should make sure that the target has been characterized fully. If the attacker has not gained an in-depth understanding of the network, there is a high likelihood that the attack will fully fail. Also, the attacker can be easily detected.
- The attacker should first look into whether the exploit is well known. Are there some actions that have already been defined in the system? If an exploit has not been fully characterized, there might be some consequences that are unintended. It is good to make sure that all exploits have been validated first.
- First look into the manner in which the exploit is being carried out. For instance, the attack may be conducted from a remote location and that means that you cannot be caught easily. The main issue is that you will not have a lot of control over the exploits.
- Consider some of the post-exploit activities. If you need to gather some data first, you must make sure that you have established some interactive actions.

Consider whether you should maintain access or whether you will be compromised. Such factors will help to ensure that you have come up with a stealthy approach to avoid detection.

There are many vulnerabilities that can be easily identified. Some of these exploits are based on different techniques and that is why the system can be compromised easily. We will now provide some real examples on how to hack using Kali Linux.

Threat Modelling

The pilot study comes in handy and it makes sure that you can learn more about the present vulnerabilities. Always make sure that the attack has been coordinated in a planned manner. If not, you may fail to achieve your objectives. Also, you can be caught easily. When carrying out an attack, there is a process commonly referred to as threat modelling. It is good to note that the attackers and testers are using the same tools. The main difference is the motive of each party.

Threat modelling comes in handy when trying to improve the success rate of an attack. There is the offensive threat modelling and it involves the use of the research and the results of the pilot study. As an attacker, you must first consider the availability of targets. The types of targets are as shown in the list below:

Primary targets- when such a target is compromised, they will support the objective.

Secondary targets- this is a target who can provide some information such as passwords and security controls. The information will come in handy when launching an attack.

Tertiary targets- these are targets that can be compromised easily and they can also be distracted easily and that means that they can also provide some information that can be used to launch an attack.

For every target, the attacker should always determine the approach that they want to use. If there are some vulnerabilities, the attacker will go ahead and launch the attack. If there is a large-scale attack, some issues may occur. Some attackers make use of the attack tree methodology. The following diagram will provide some overview about the attack tree methodology:

The approach is used when trying to visualize some attack options that will ensure that the attack has gone accordingly. After generating an attack tree, you can visualize the attack options that are available. The vulnerabilities will ensure that you have learned more about the most suitable attack options.

How to Use the Vulnerability Resources

The pilot study helps you to learn more about the target's attack surface and that means it is the total number of points that you will assess to find the vulnerabilities. If a server has an operating system, it means that the server can only be exploited if the operating system has some vulnerabilities. If many applications have been installed into the system, there will be many vulnerabilities.

As an attacker, you will be tasked with finding some of the vulnerabilities that are present within the system. For starters, you should make sure that you have looked into some of the vendor sites. You will gain access to some information about different vulnerabilities and the period when some patches and upgrades have been released. There are some exploits for different weaknesses and they are commonly known. There are many vendors who will provide some of this information to their clients. When attackers gain access to such information, they will use it to their own advantage. You can gain access to this information from numerous sources.

Kali Linux has an exploit database. It is situated in the /usr/share/exploitdb directory. Before you can use it, you should update it using the following command:

Start by opening a terminal window by searching for the exploitdb local copy. You will then keyin the searchsploit in the command prompt. A script will then search the database that possesses the list of all the exploits. You can then extract the exploits, compile, and run them depending on the present vulnerabilities. The following screenshot showcases some vulnerabilities.

Open a terminal window so that you can search the exploitdb. After opening a terminal window, you can key in the searchsploit command. You will then key in the search term that you want to look up. A script will be invoked and a database will all the exploits will appear. The files will be in the .csv format. The search allows you to learn about different vulnerabilities. You can also extract the exploits, and later compile and run them against various vulnerabilities. The screenshot below showcases a list if various vulnerabilities:

When searching the local database, you will realize that there are many exploits that are present within the system. The path listing will also list some descriptions. You must also make sure that the environment has been customized before you can launch an attack. There are some exploits that are presented in the form of scripts and they include PHP, Perl, and Ruby. Some of these exploits can be implemented easily. If you want to hack into a server such as the Microsoft II 6.0, such an exploit is easy since the server can be accessed remotely using the WebDAV. To exploit the server, you should by copying the exploit and then copying it into the root directory. You will then execute the exploit using a Perl script as shown below:

Some of these exploits are in the form of source codes that should be compiled before you can use them. For instance, if you are searching for the RPC vulnerabilities, you will realize that there are many vulnerabilities. An example is shown in the screenshot below:

There are many vulnerabilities including RPC DCOM. It is normally identified as a 76.c When compiling this exploit, you will start by copying it from the storage directory into the /tmp directory. Within the specified location, you will then compile everything using the command that is shown below:

The 76.c will then be compiled using the GNU compiler. The screenshot below will offer some guidance:

After invoking the application depending on your target, you should make sure that you have called the executable using the following command:

As for this exploit, the source code has been well documented and you should also adhere to some parameters that are quite clear during the execution process. The screenshot below has offered some guidance:

Although there are many exploits, not all of these exploits will exploit the public resources or the database that has been compiled as a 76.c. There are numerous issues that are present and that is why using some of these exploits becomes a problematic affair. Some of the issues include:

The source code may be incomplete and some deliberate errors may also be present as some of the developers try to make sure that some of these exploits cannot be utilized by some users that are not experienced. Some of these beginners may be trying to compromise the system and they may not be conversant with some of the involved risks depending on their specific actions.

Some of these exploits have not been documented in a comprehensive manner and that means that the way in which the use of the source code is used may bring about some issues. If an attacker or a tester encounters some issues, they will not be able to make good use of these exploits.

The changing environments will bring about some inconsistent behavior and that means that the source code will be changed significantly. Only as skilled developer should handle such a task.

Some of the source codes may contain some malicious functionalities and the attacker may use this to their own advantage when trying to penetrate a system. The malicious functionalities come in handy when trying to create a backdoor that will allow them to enter into the system as they wish.

As an attacker, you will want to make sure that your results are consistent and that is why some coders have come together to form a community. They are able to come up with different practices that are also consistent. Some of the suitable exploitation frameworks include the Metasploit framework.

The Metasploit Framework

The Metasploit framework is in the form of an open source tool that has been designed to facilitate the penetration into a network. The framework was created using the Ruby programming language. A modular approach was used during the creation process and that is why people can easily code and develop different exploits. Some complex tasks can be easily be implemented using the Metasploit framework.

The Metasploit framework will always present numerous interfaces to each of the backend modules and it will be easy to control the entire exploitation process. As for this case, we will make use of the console interface since it guarantees high speeds. Also, the interface will present some attack commands and people can also easily understand the interface. You should start by opening the command prompt and after that you will key in the msfconsole.

The Metasploit framework has many modules that have been combined together to affect an exploit. The modules include:

Exploits: the fragments of the code that are normally used to target different vulnerabilities. Some of these active exploits will focus on a specific target. They will run and after that they will exit. As for the passive explots, they only act when a user has connected to a network.

Payloads: the payloads are in the form of malicous codes that normally implement some commands after an exploit has been carried out successfully.

- Post modules- after an attack has been perforemed successfully, the modules will run on some of the targets that have been compromised. Some important data will then be collected and the atacker will gain some deeper access into the network.

- Auxiliary modules- some of these modules do not allow some access between the attacker and the target system. The modules perform some activities such as fuzzing, scanning, or sniffing.
- Encoders- some of the exploits can bypass some of the antivirus defenses. The modules can be used to encode the payload and it will not be able to detect the techniques that are used to match signatures.
- No operations- these modules are used to facilitate the overflow of buffers during an attack.

When performing a pilot study, you may make use of some of these modules. If you want to use the Metasploit framework when performing an attack, you can follow some of these steps:

1. You will choose an exploit and comfigure it. The configired code will be used to compromise the system depending on the present vulnerabilities.
2. You will then check the target system so that you may determine whether it is vulnerable to an attack.

3. Choosing and configuring the payload.
4. You will choose an encoding technique so that you may bypass th detection controls.
5. Execute an exploit.

Exploiting Vulnerable Applications

The Metasploit framework has come in handy when exploiting some of the vulnerabilities that are present in some of the third-party applications. In this instance, we will look into how the buffer overflow can be exploited. For starters, the vulnerabilities woll be present in the ReadFile function and it is used to store the user data that has not been stored securely. When initiating the attack, the tester will have to generate the BMP file that has been specially crafted. The target will then open the file when using the Chasys application. When such an acitivity occuers, the base operating system will be compromised. The attack is effective on operating systems such as XP service pack 3 and Windows 7 service pack 1.

To initiate the attack, open the msfconsole. The Metasploit will then be used to perform the exploit as shown below:

The exploit is quite simple; however, the attacker should set a reverse shell to the target system. They should also make sure that the system has been compromised. After the exploit is complete, a BMP file will then be created and it will be stored with the name msf.bmp by default. The attacker should make sure that they have enticed the target so that they may open the file. To do so, the attacker should make sure that the file has not been stored using the default name since it may also be detected by different devices. The name should be changed to something that may be relevant to the target. After that, the attacker should then launch a new instance of the msfconsole. A listener will also be set up to keep track of the reverse TCP shell since it will originate from the target's end after they have been compromised. The following screenshot shows a simple listener.

After the target has opened the BMP image file that is present in the vulnerable application. , there will be a meterpreter session that will be established in both systems. The meterpreter prompt will then replace the msf prompt. The attacker will not be able to access the system remotely using the command shell. The first step after ensuring that the system has been compromised is to verify that the system is accessible. The screenshot below showcases the operating system and the computer name after the attacker keys in the sysinfo command into the terminal window:

How to Exploit Numerous Targets When Using Armitage

Armitage's functionality can be likened to the Metasploit console. When using Armitage, you have access to numerous options that come in handy when attacking some targets that have various complexities. The main advantage of using Armitage is that you can exploit multiple targets at once. The maximum number of targets that you can exploit in one instance is 512.

Before starting Armitage, you must make sure that the Metasploit services and the database are up and running. You should use the following command:

You will then type ARMITAGE in the command prompt so that you can execute the command. There are some steps that you should follow when launching Armitage so that it can function accordingly. So that you can discover the targets that are available, you will have to provide an IP address so that you can add a host. You can also enumerate targets when using Armitage since it will use DNS enumeration.

When using Armitage, you can also import some data that is present in files such as amap, Acunetix, Burp proxy, AppScan, Nessus NBE, Foundstine, and XML files.You can also set a host label when using Armitage. You will start by right-clicking so that you may select a host. You will then go to the host menu where you will set the host label. You can then flag a particular IP address. The following screenshot can offer some guidance:

Armitage has also been supporting dynamic workspaces. You may start by testing a network while also trying to identify some of the servers that have not been patched. You can highlight all these servers by issuing a label and then placing all of them in a workspace that has been prioritized. After identifying some targets, you can then select some modules that can be implemented during the exploitation phase. There is also an attack option in the menu bar.

When exploiting a host, you can right-click and navigate to the attack item while also choosing an exploit.

Always make sure that you have chosen the right operating system to ensure that the exploit is successful. There is the Hail Mary option. It is present in the Attacks option. When you select this function, you will view all the systems that have been identified and they can be subjected automatically to some of the exploits that can enable an attacker to learn more about a huge number of compromises. Such an attack is quite noisy.

If a system has been compromised, it will appear as an icon and it will have a red border. Some electrical sparks will also be present. In the screenshot that will be displayed here, there will be two compromised systems. There will also be a total of four active sessions.

As an attacker, you must make sure that you have looked into all the present vulnerabilities. In the screenshot above, the Hail Mary Option has showcased that there are two vulnerabilities and there are two active sessions. When carrying out manual testing using a similar target, more vulnerabilities will appear. When carrying out real-world tests, you will realize that there are some advantages and disadvantages of using automated tools.

Network Exploitation

When hacking with Kali Linux, you can easily exploit a network. You can use some of the tools present within the operating system to find some of the vulnerabilities that are present in a network. In this section, we will focus more on the ways through which you can carry out a penetration test on a network while also exploiting different services.

Man, in the Middle Attack Using Ferret and Hamster

The hamster tool comes in handy when carrying out side jacking. The tools usually acts as a proxy server. Ferret is used to sniff for cookies in a network. In this context, we will learn more about how to hack into a network.

Getting Ready

The Kali Linux operating system has many tools that are already pre-installed. Since we are looking into network exploitation, we will now look into how you can use some of these tools.

The Hamster tool is easy to use and it also has its own user interface. To learn more about hamster, you should follow the following steps.

1. You will start by keying in the following command in the terminal window;

```
hamster
```

The output of the 'hamster' command is as shown below:

2. You will then start the browser and try to navigate http://localhost:1234:

Now we just need to fire up our browser and navigate to

3. *We will then click on one of the adapters and then choose the specific interface that we will monitor:*

4. *After some few minutes, the sessions will appear on the left-hand side of the browser tab.*

In some instances, the sessions may fail to appear. In such an instance, you should exercise some patience since the ferret and hamster tools are not located in the same folder. Hamster usually runs while also executing ferret in the background. The main issue with ferret is that it is not suited to being used with the 64-bit architecture. If you are using the 64-but Kali Linux version, you must make sure that you have added the 32-bit repository first. After that, you can install ferret. You should use the following command:

How to explore the msfconsole

It is good to learn about the basics of the Metasploit; however, in this case, we will just learn more about how you can use Metasploit when carrying out an attack.

If you want to learn about Metasploit, the following tips will come in handy:

1. *You should type msfconsole so that you can start the Metasploit console.*

2. There are many exploits available and you can view them using the following command

The output of the command is as shown below:

3. If you want to see the current payloads, you should use the following command:

The output of the command is as shown below:

4. Metasploit has many modules and they contain fuzzers, scanners, sniffers, and many more modules. You can see the auxiliary modules using the following command:

The output of the above command is shown below:

5. If you want to use the FTP fuzzer command, you should use the following command:

6. To see the available options, use the following command:

7. You can use the following command to set the RHOSTS:

8. There is the auxiliary that notifies you that a crash has taken place and you should always run it.

The Railgun in Metasploit

In this section, the main focus will be on the Railgun. It is a meterpreter and it is the only feature that can be used to exploit Windows. You can use it to communicate directly with the Windows API.

When using Railgun, you can perform various tasks that the Metasploit cannot including pressing keyboard keys. The Windows API will enable you to perform the exploitation in a better manner.

1. To run the Railgun, you should key in the irb command in the terminal window.

2. If you want to access the Railgyun, you should key in the session.railgun command in the terminal window.

As per the screenshot above, there is a lot of data that has been printed. There are many functions and DLL's that we can utilize.

> 1. If you want to see the DLL names, you should key in the following command:

The output is as shown below:

1. To view a function of a .dll, we use the following command:

```
session.railgun.<dllname>.functions
```

The following screenshot shows the output for the preceding command:

```
>> session.railgun.kernel32.functions
=> {"GetConsoleWindow"=>#<Rex::Post::Meterpreter::Extensions::Stdapi::Railgun::D
LLFunction:0x000000054088c8 @return_type="LPVOID", @params=[], @windows_name="Ge
tConsoleWindow", @calling_conv="stdcall">, "ActivateActCtx"=>#<Rex::Post::Meterp
reter::Extensions::Stdapi::Railgun::DLLFunction:0x00000005543288 @return_type="B
OOL", @params=[["HANDLE", "hActCtx", "inout"], ["PBLOB", "lpCookie", "out"]], @w
indows_name="ActivateActCtx", @calling_conv="stdcall">, "AddAtomA"=>#<Rex::Post:
:Meterpreter::Extensions::Stdapi::Railgun::DLLFunction:0x00000005542b30 @return
```

2. We can then call an API that will be used to lock the target's screen. We will use the following command:

We were able to lock the screen of the target using the API as shown below:

3. When exploiting a network, we can also gain access to the login passwords of the target user. First, we must have the hash. We will then crack it. Also, note that we are running Kali Linux on the "Live mode" and we can also access Windows using an API so that it may

be easy to perform a penetration test. Depending on the results of the test, you can go ahead and exploit the present vulnerabilities. The Windows API can come in handy when you want to run a keylogger. When the user keys in the logins, you will have access to the passwords. The main advantage is that Metasploit also has a module and it also uses Railgun when trying to retrieve the target's passwords.

4. We will start by exiting irb and the meterpreter session will then start to run in the background. We will use the following command:

The command will give us the following output:

5. To add a session, you will make use of the set session command.

6. We will then set the PID using the following command:

7. After running the command, it is possible to see the password that the user has keyed in:

We have just issued an example. Railgun can be used to perform any more actions including creating DLLs and also deleting different users.

How to Use the Paranoid Meterpreter

Apparently, you can also hack into someone's meterpreter session. The attacker should just play around with the DNS of the target and they will connect after launching their own handler. To ensure that an attack could take place swiftly, the meterpreter paranoid mode was developed and released. An API was also introduced and it could be used to verify the SHA1 hash of any of the certificates that had been presented by the msf. We will now learn more about how to use the meterpreter paranoid mode.

For starters, we will need an SSL certificate.

1. You can generate some SSL certificates using the commands shown below:

The output of the command is as shown below:

```
root@kali:~/Desktop# openssl req -new -newkey rsa:4096 -days 365 -nodes -x509
eyout meterpreter.key -out meterpreter.crt
Generating a 4096 bit RSA private key
.........................++
...............................................................................
.......++
writing new private key to 'meterpreter.key'
.....
You are about to be asked to enter information that will be incorporated
into your certificate request.
What you are about to enter is what is called a Distinguished Name or a DN.
There are quite a few fields but you can leave some blank
For some fields there will be a default value,
If you enter '.', the field will be left blank.
.....
Country Name (2 letter code) [AU]:IN
```

You will have to fill in some information such as the
country code after keying in the command shown
below:

> 2. The first command in this section is used to
>   open two files and then it writes both of them
>   into a single file. To generate a payload using
>   the certificate that has been generated, we
>   will use the following command:

The output of the command is shown in the screenshot
below:

> 3. If you want to set the options, you will use
>   this command:

The preceding command is shown in the screenshot below:

4. We will then run the handler. In this stage, the connection will have been verified by the stager and a connection will have been established.

The tale of the bleeding heart

This is a vulnerability that is present in the OpenSSL cryptography. It had been introduced in 2012; however, the public came to learn about it in 2012. This is a vulnerability where an attacker can gain access to more data than is allowed. In this section, we will look into how to use the Metasploit to exploit the bleeding heart

The following steps will make sure that you have learned more about the bleeding heart.

1. To start the msfconsole, we will use the following command:

The output that you should expect is as shown in the screenshot below:

2. You will then use the following command to search for the HeartBleed auxiliary:

The output to expect is as shown in the screenshot below:

3. To use the auxiliary, you should use the following command:

4. The following command will allow us to see the available options:

The output will be as shown in the screenshot below:

5. The following command will allow us to set the RHOSTS to a specific IP address:

6. To set the verbosity, we will use the following command and it should be set to true:

```
set verbose true
```

7. We will type run so that we may see the data and it normally contains some sensitive information including email IDs and passwords.

11. Cryptography And Network Security

With a rapid increase in the rate of cyber attacks, it is of utter importance to protect all forms of confidential data as much as possible. Data leakage can lead to serious loss for various businesses and can also turn out to be a threat for an individual person where the credit card, as well as bank details, are breached. The term cryptography is linked with the technique used for converting plain and ordinary text into unintelligible form. With this method, transmission and storage of sensitive data become a lot easier. Only those to whom the message is intended can process the text and read it. It is not only helpful in protecting data from breaching or theft but it is also useful for data authentication.

In the world of computer science, cryptography is associated with securing all forms of information along with the techniques of communication which are derived from the concepts of mathematics. It uses a definite set of ruled calculations which are known as algorithms. The algorithms are used for transforming the messages in such a way that it becomes very hard to decipher the same. Such algorithms of deterministic character are used in the generation of cryptographic keys along with digital signing for protecting the privacy of data, browsing various websites on the internet and for sensitive communications like email and credit card or bank transaction details.

Techniques of cryptography

The technique of cryptography is often linked with the characteristics of cryptanalysis and cryptology. The technique of cryptography includes the usage of various techniques like merging of words with various images, microdots and several other techniques which are used for hiding that information which is in transit or in storage. However, in the world of computer today, the technique of cryptography is often linked with the process of scrambling ordinary text or cleartext. Such form of ordinary text is known as plaintext. The plaintext is converted into ciphertext with the process of encryption and then back to the original form with the help of decryption. The people who specialize in the field of cryptography are called cryptographers.

Objectives of cryptography

The modern-day objectives of cryptography are as follows:

- Confidentiality: Confidentiality is the act of keeping all forms of personal and sensitive data protected for the concerned people. The information which is being transmitted or stored cannot be analyzed or understood by any third party for whom it was not at all intended.

- Integrity: The data or information which is being transmitted or stored cannot be changed or altered between the sender and the receiver who is intended to receive the data. In case any form of alteration is made, the sender and receiver will both be notified.

- Non-repudiation: The sender, as well as the creator of the data or information, will not be allowed to deny his/her intentions at a later stage during the creation or transportation of the data or information.

- Authentication: Both the parties in communication who are the sender and the receiver will have the capability of confirming the identity of each other along with the origin and final destination of the data.

The protocols and the procedures that meet all of the mentioned objectives and criteria are called cryptosystems. The cryptosystems are often taken as only referring to the procedure of mathematics and programs of computer only. However, in actual, they also comprise of human behavior regulation like logging off from the systems which are not used, choosing strong and difficult to guess passwords while logging in and not discussing any form of sensitive data and procedure with the outside world.

Algorithms of cryptography

The cryptosystems work along with a bunch of procedures called ciphers or cryptographic algorithms. It is being used for the purpose of encrypting as well as for decrypting the messages for securing up the communications among smartphones, applications and other computer systems. A suite of cipher uses up one single algorithm for the purpose of encryption, one more algorithm for authentication of messages and another algorithm for exchange of keys. This whole process is embedded within the protocols and is written within the programming of software which runs on the OS along with the computer systems which are based on the network. It also involves generation of public as well as private key for the process of encryption as well as decryption of data, verification for the purpose of message authentication, digital signing along with the exchange of keys.

Cryptography and its types

There are various types of cryptography which are being used today.

- Encryption using single key or symmetric key: The algorithms of this form of cryptography create block cipher which are actually particular length of bits. The block cipher comes along with one secret key that the sender uses for encrypting the data. The same key can be used by the receiver for deciphering the information. AES or Advanced Encryption Standard is a type of symmetric key encryption which was launched by the

NIST as Federal Information Processing Standard or FIPS 197 in the year 2001. It is being used for the protection of confidential and sensitive data. In the year 2003, the U.S. government approved of AES for the purpose of classified information. AES is a form of specification which is free from royalty and is used in all forms of hardware and software in the whole world. AES succeeded DES and DES3. AES uses up longer lengths of keys for preventing attacks.

- Encryption using public key or asymmetric key: The algorithms for this form of cryptography uses two keys at a time in pair. One public key which is associated along with the sender and the receiver for the purpose of encrypting the information. Another private key is used for the purpose of decryption of the message. The private key is only known to the originator. There are various forms of cryptography using public key like RSA which is used all over the internet, ECDSA which is being used by Bitcoin and DSA which has been adopted as FIPS for all forms of digital signatures by the NIST.

- Hash functions: For the purpose of maintaining the integrity of data, hash functions are used that returns an accepted value from the value which is used as input. It is being used for mapping the data into a fixed size of data. SHA-1, SHA-2 and SHA-3 are the types of hash functions.

Conclusion

Thank you for reading the Kali Linux guide to the end. I do hope the book was informative and also amusing. I also hope that you were also able to gain access to the information and tools that you needed to achieve all your goals. Although you have read the entire Hacking with Kali Linux handbook, we have not exhausted all the information that there is on Hacking with Kali Linux. You may expound on the knowledge that you possess by conducting some comprehensive research on hacking with Kali Linux.

The next step is to make sure that you can use the information in the handbook practically. You can also formulate a schedule whereby you can get to learn more about Kali Linux.

Studies have showcased that web applications, servers, and networks have vulnerabilities. As an external attacker and a penetration tester, you can make use of these vulnerabilities when launching an attack. You must also make sure that you have goals so that you may be motivated as you perform the tests and attacks.